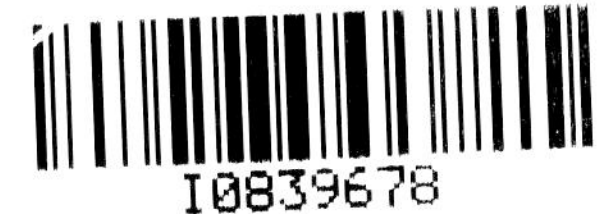
I0839678

KINGFISHER COLORING BOOK FOR ADULTS MIDNIGHT EDITION

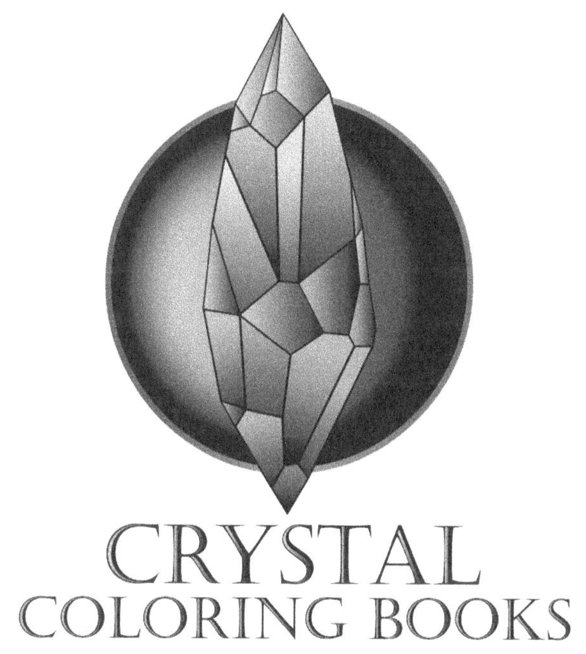

CRYSTAL
COLORING BOOKS

ISBN-13: 978-1987590517

ISBN-10: 1987590511

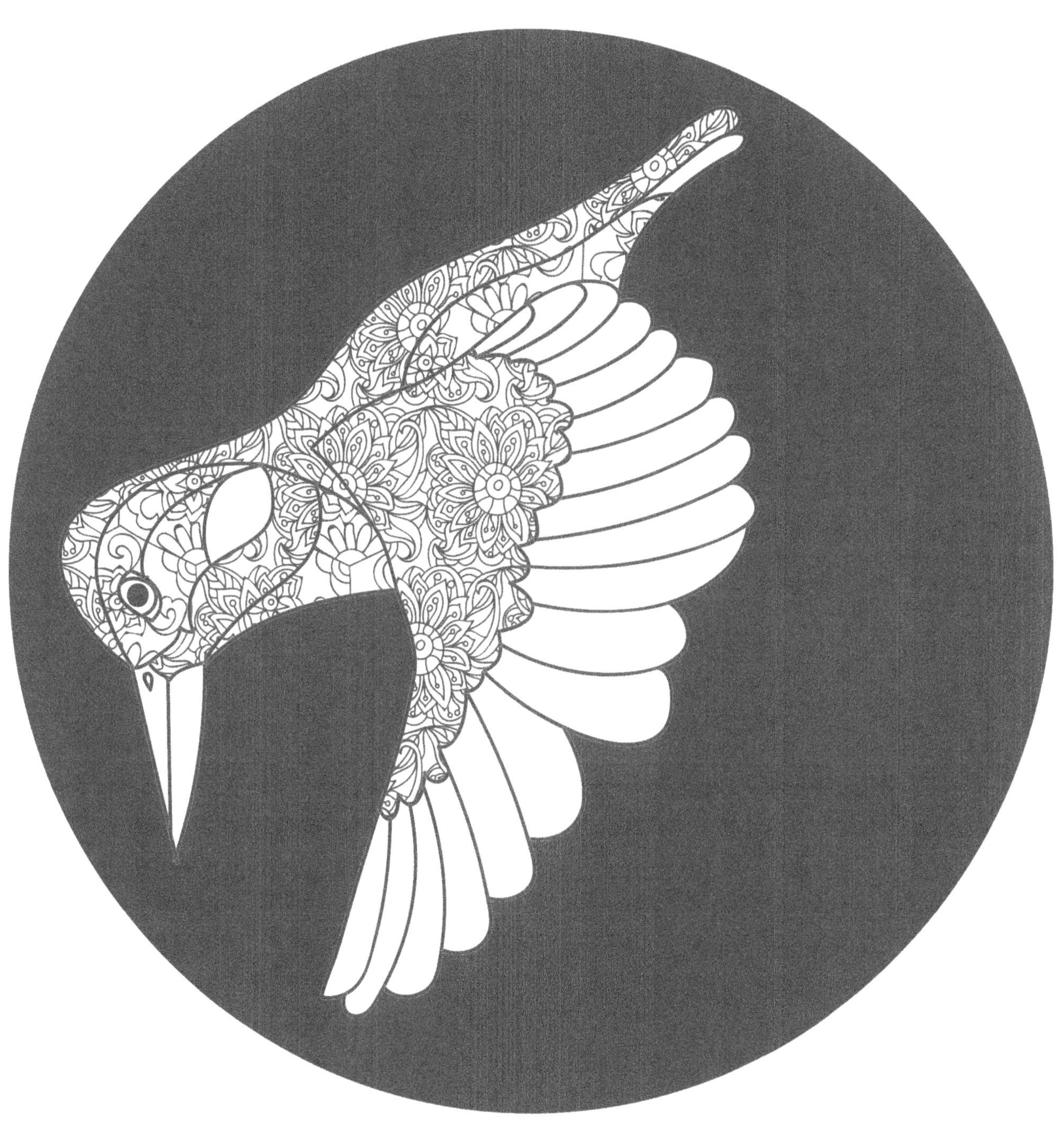

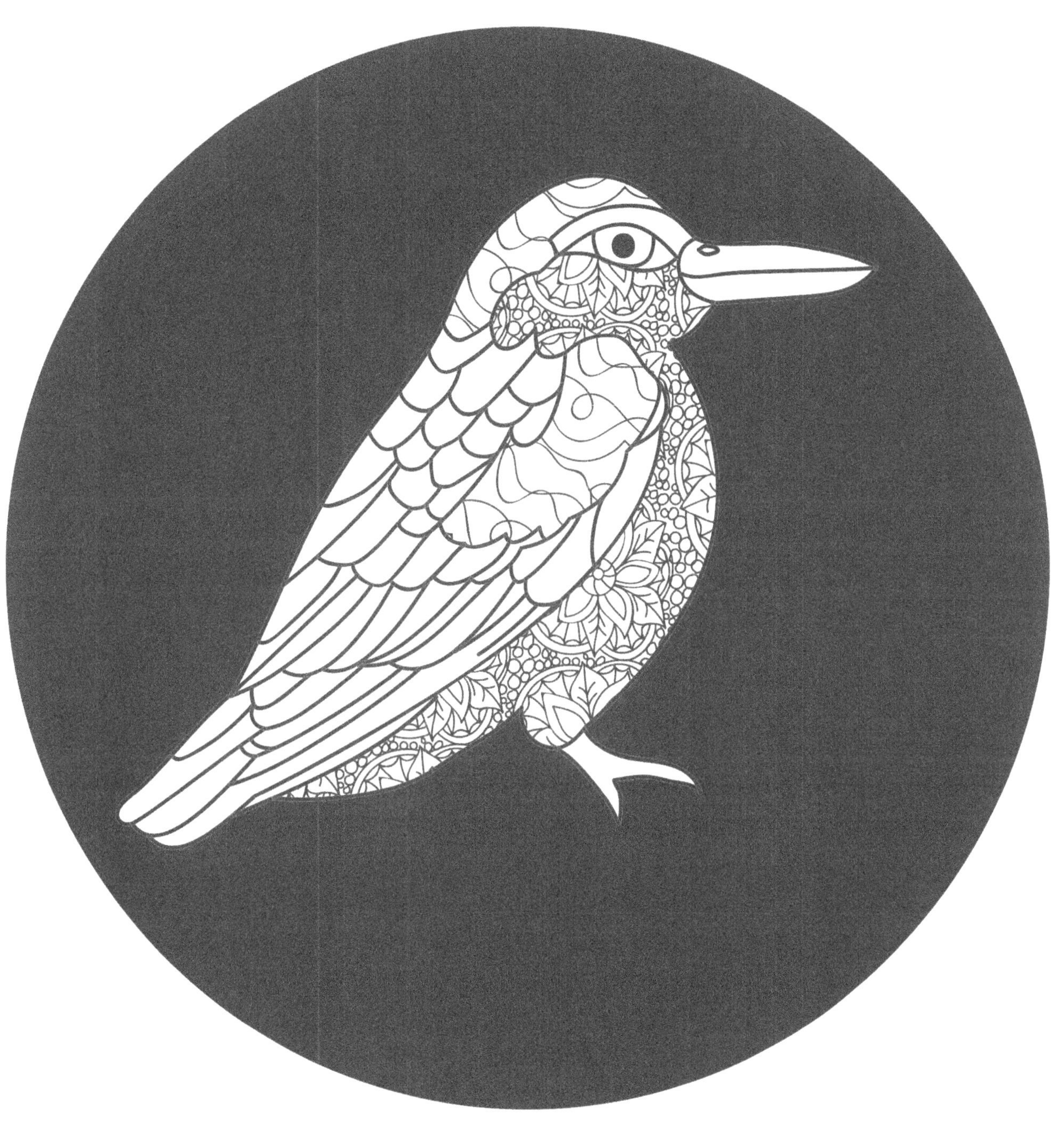

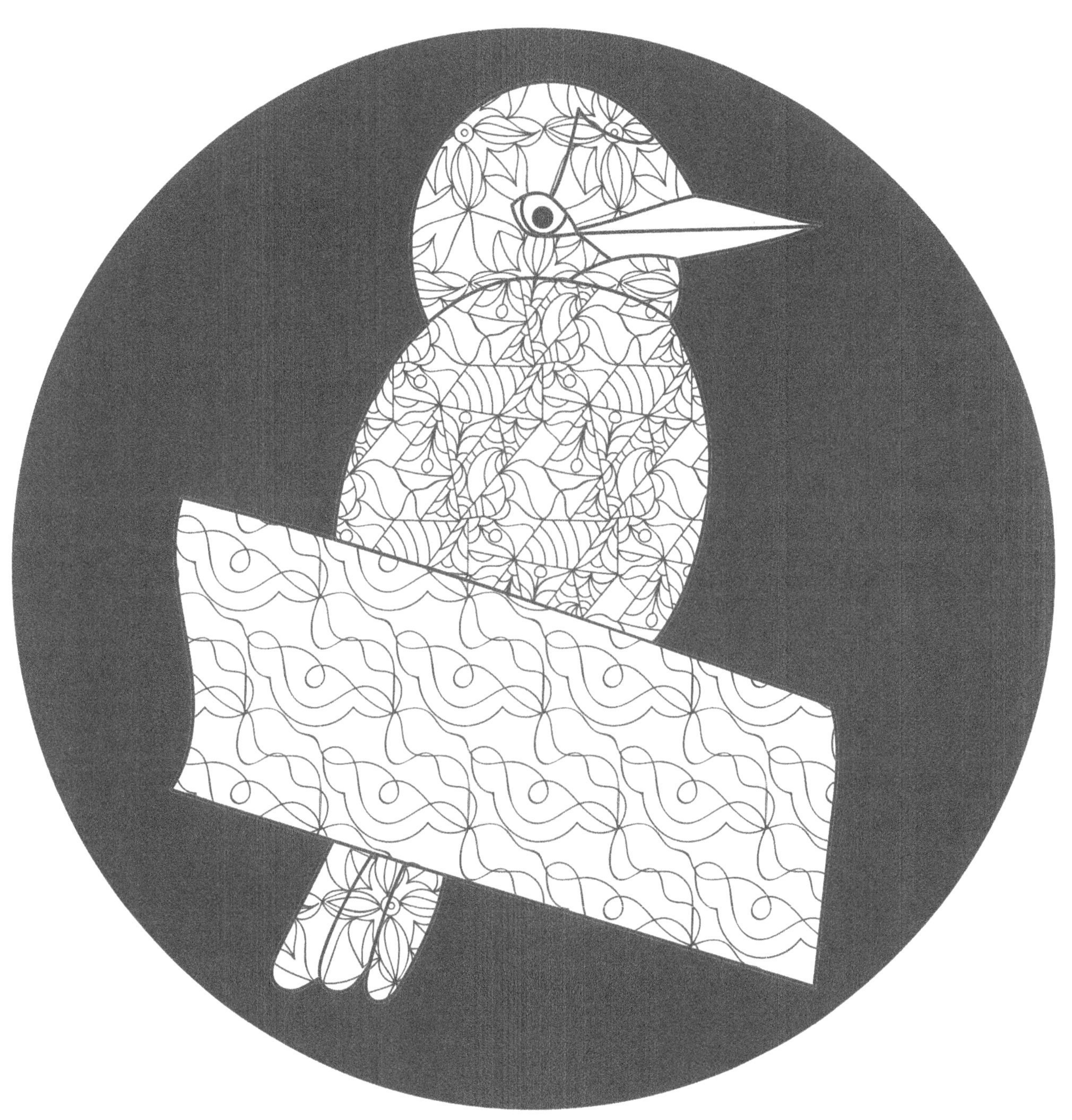

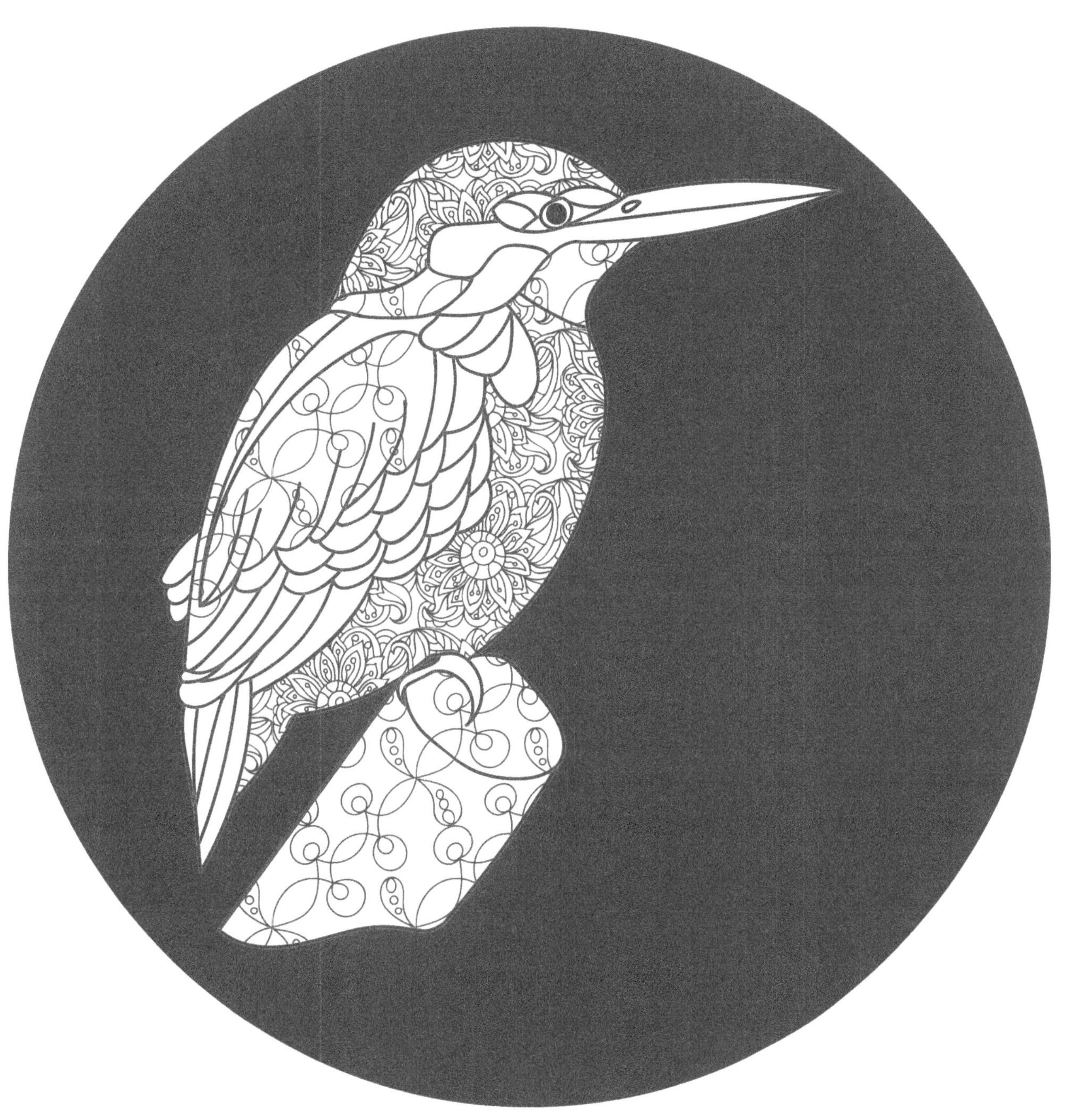

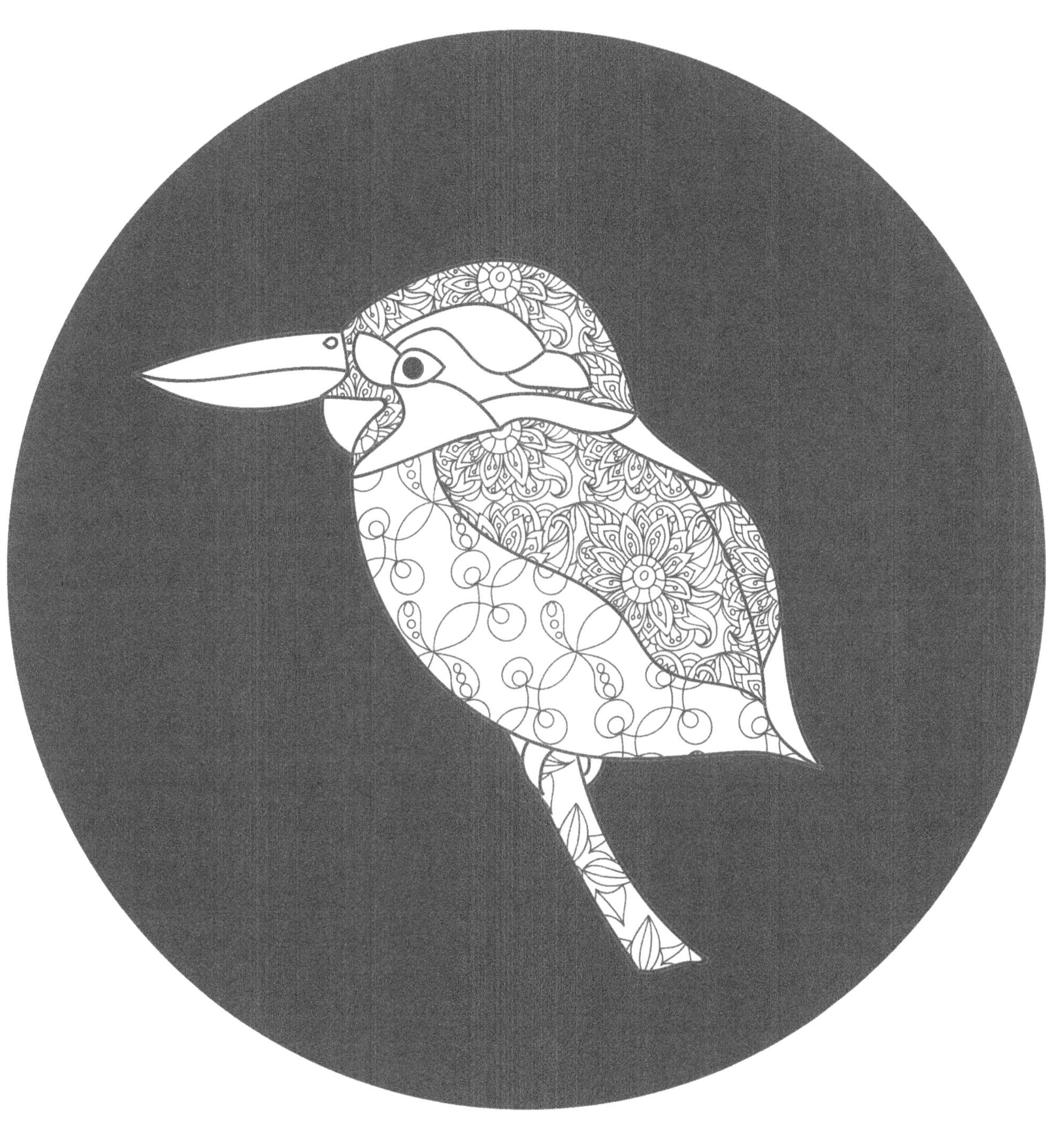

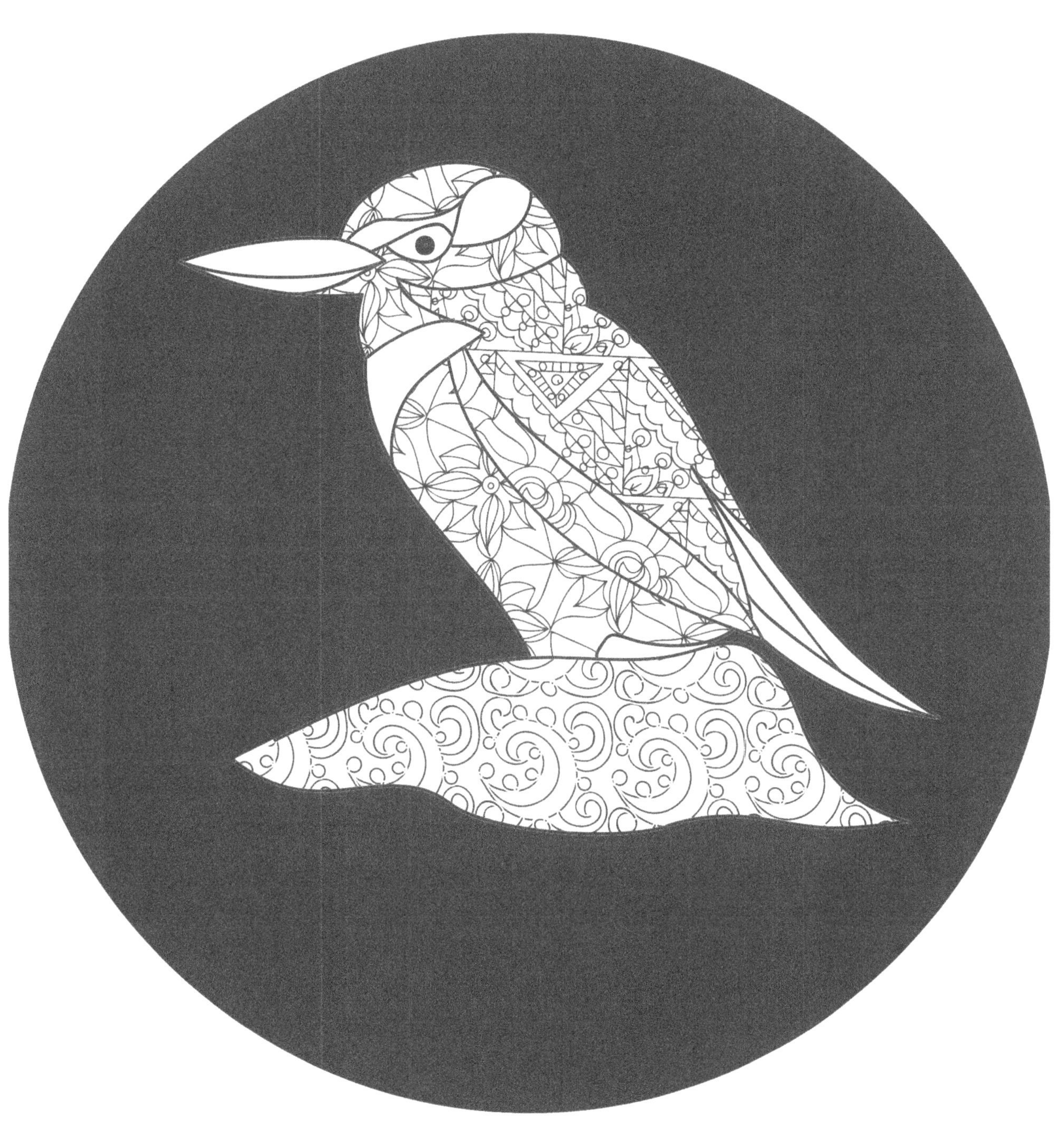

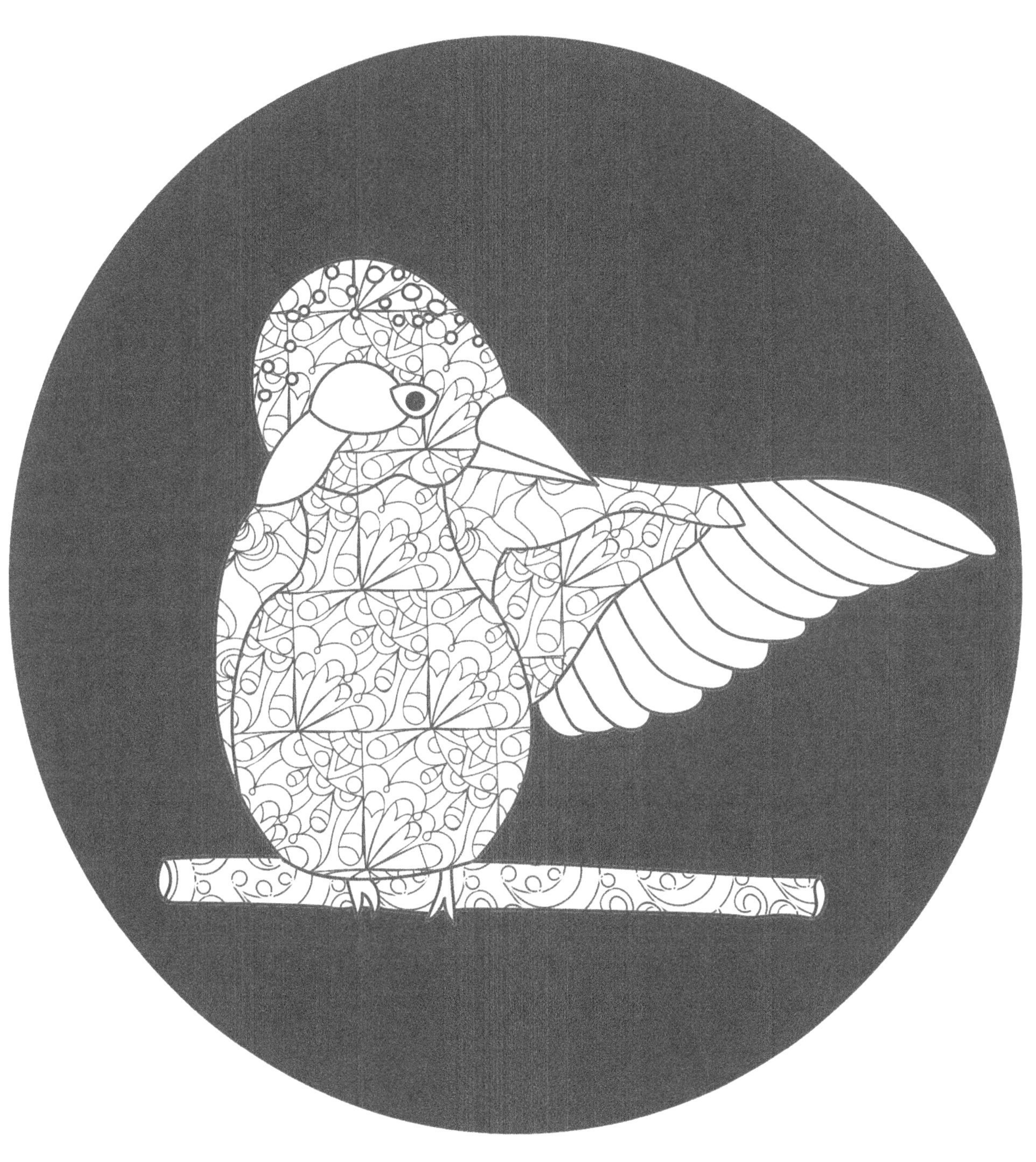

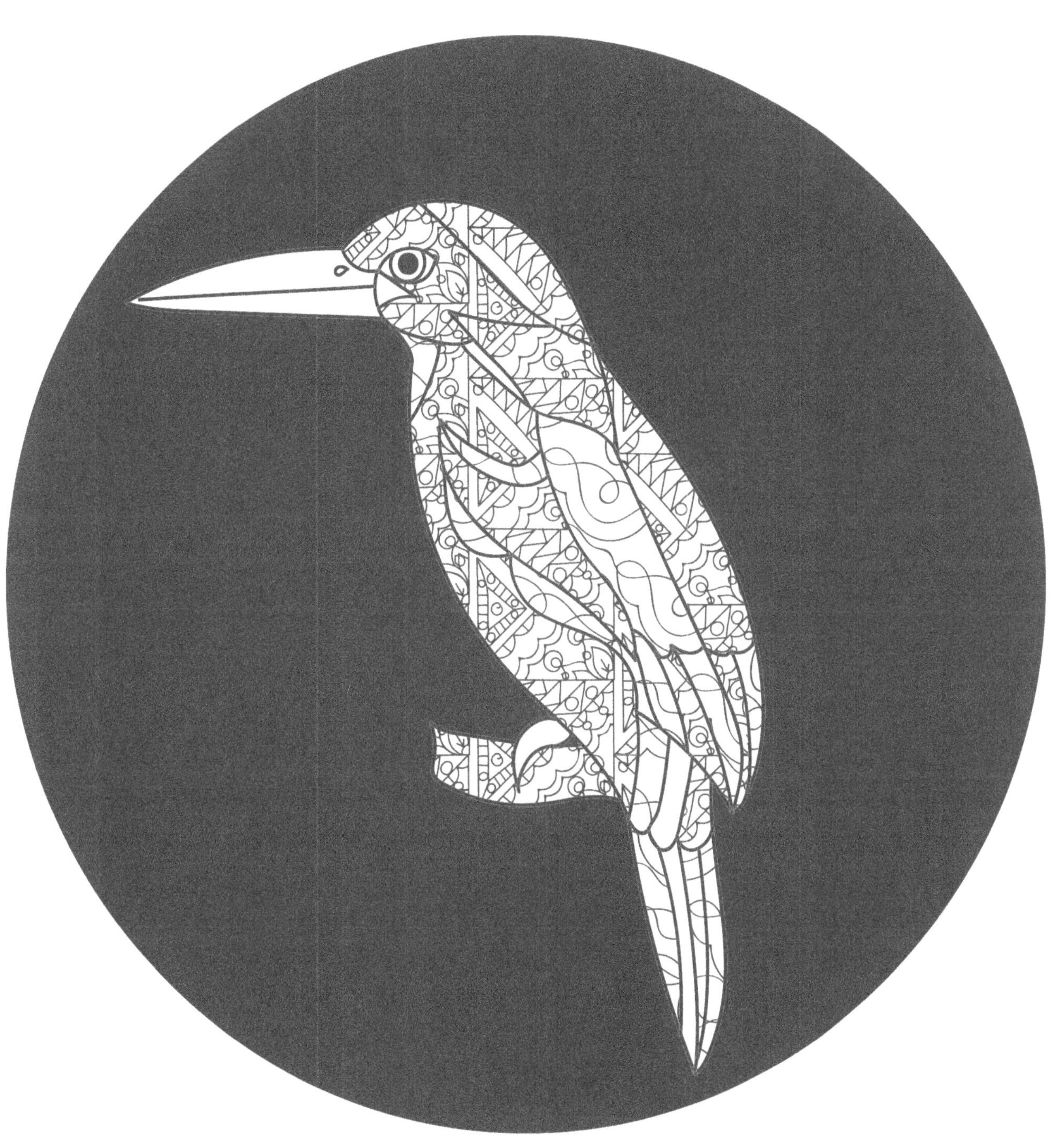

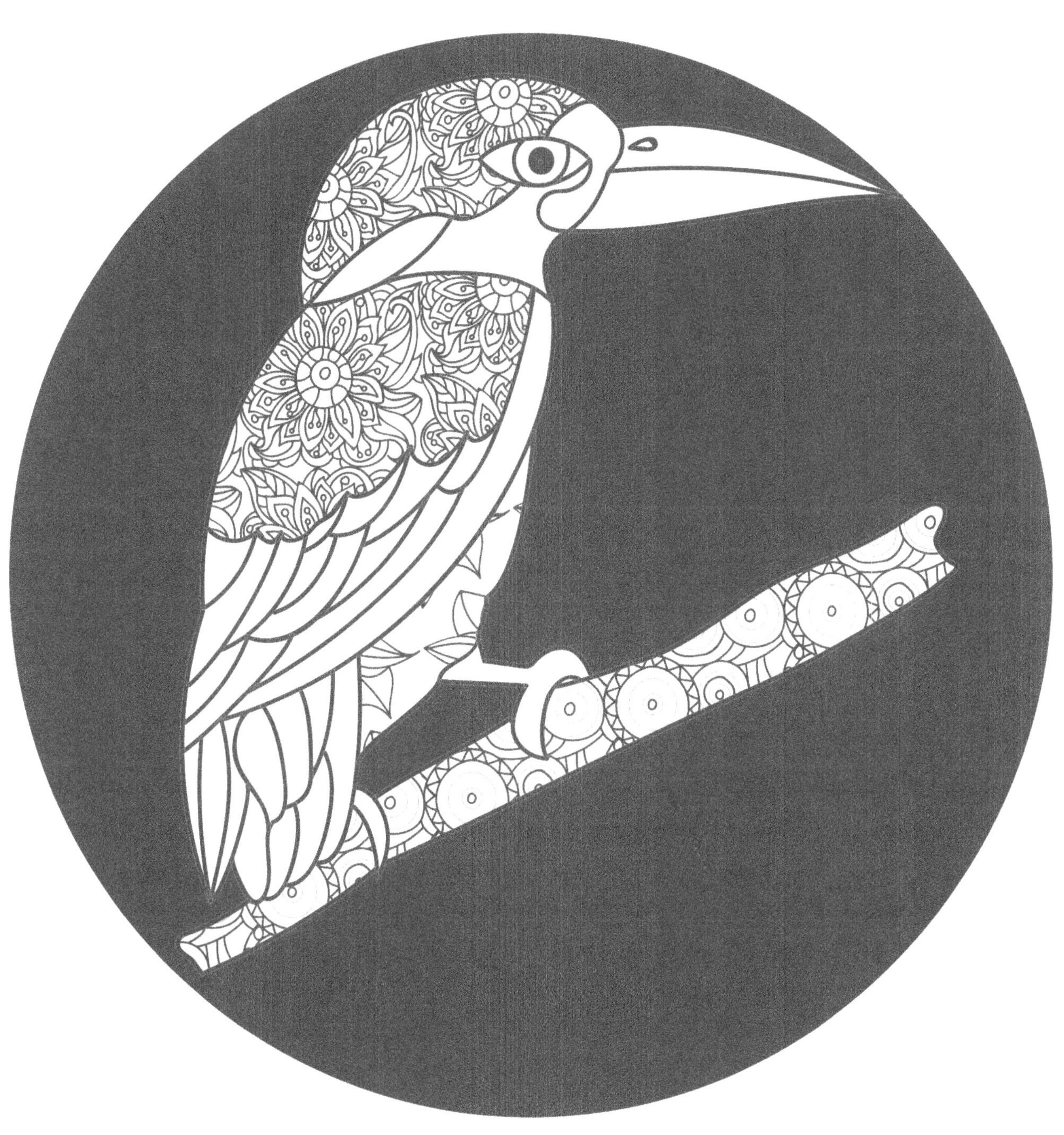

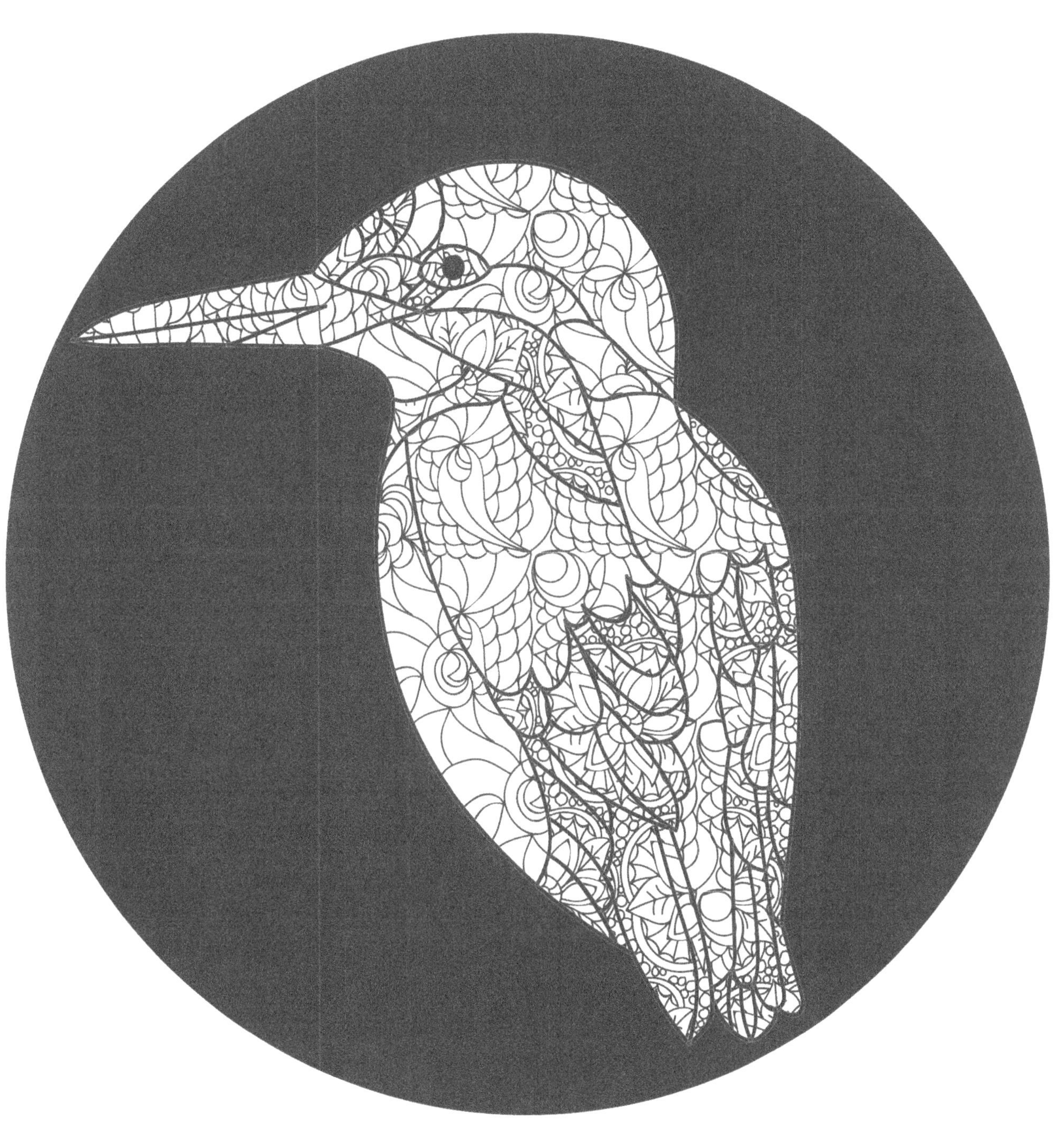

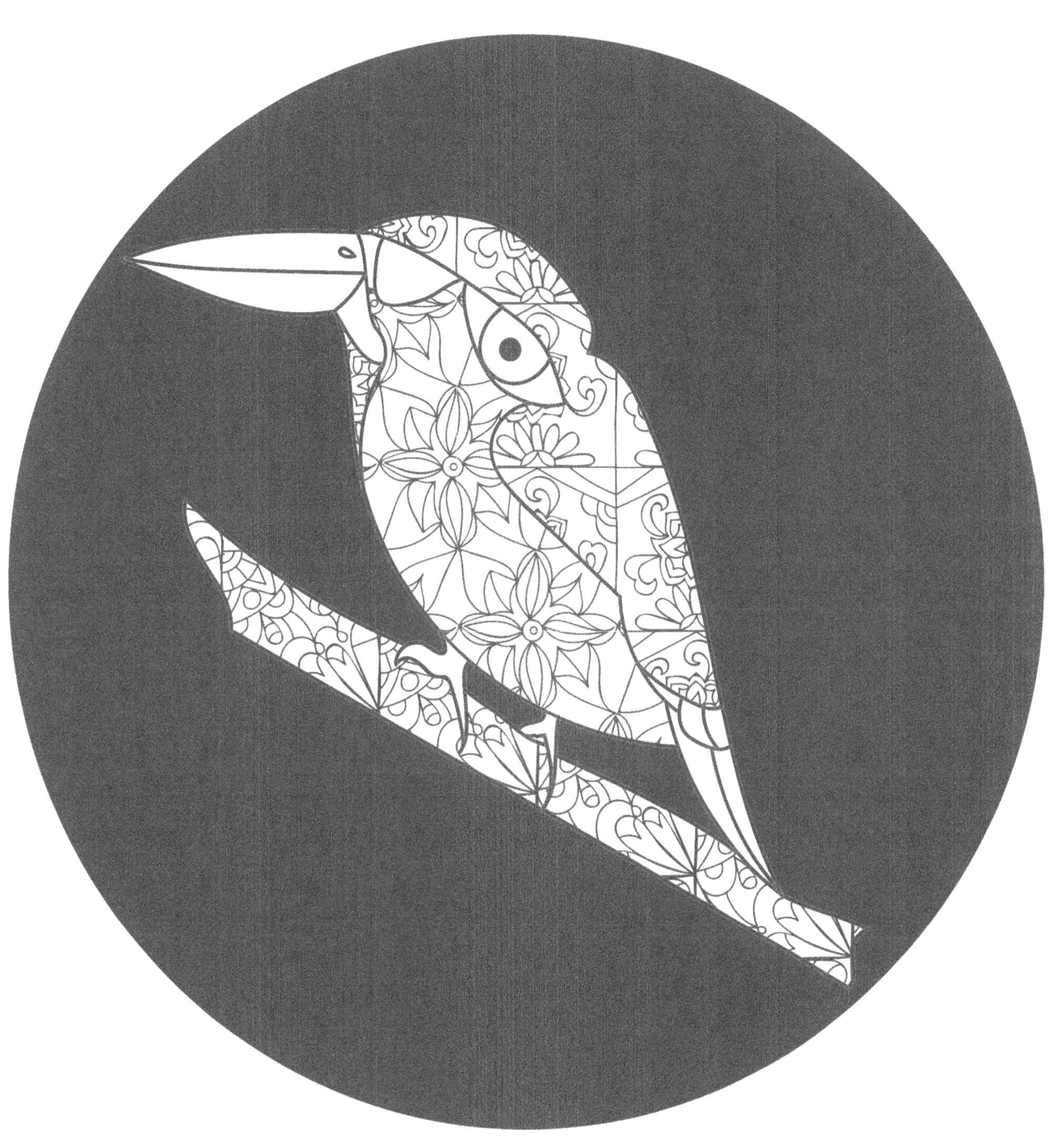

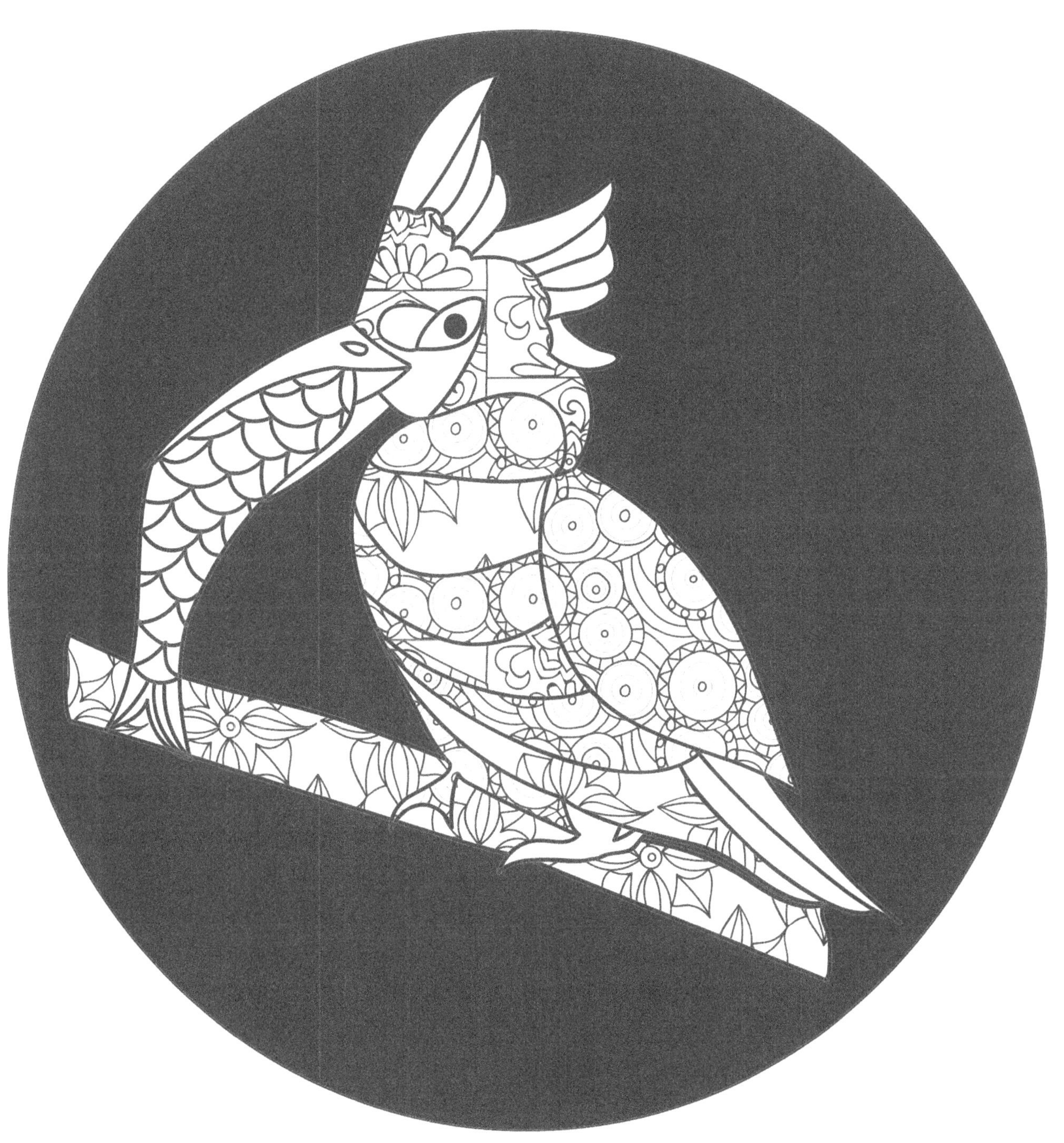

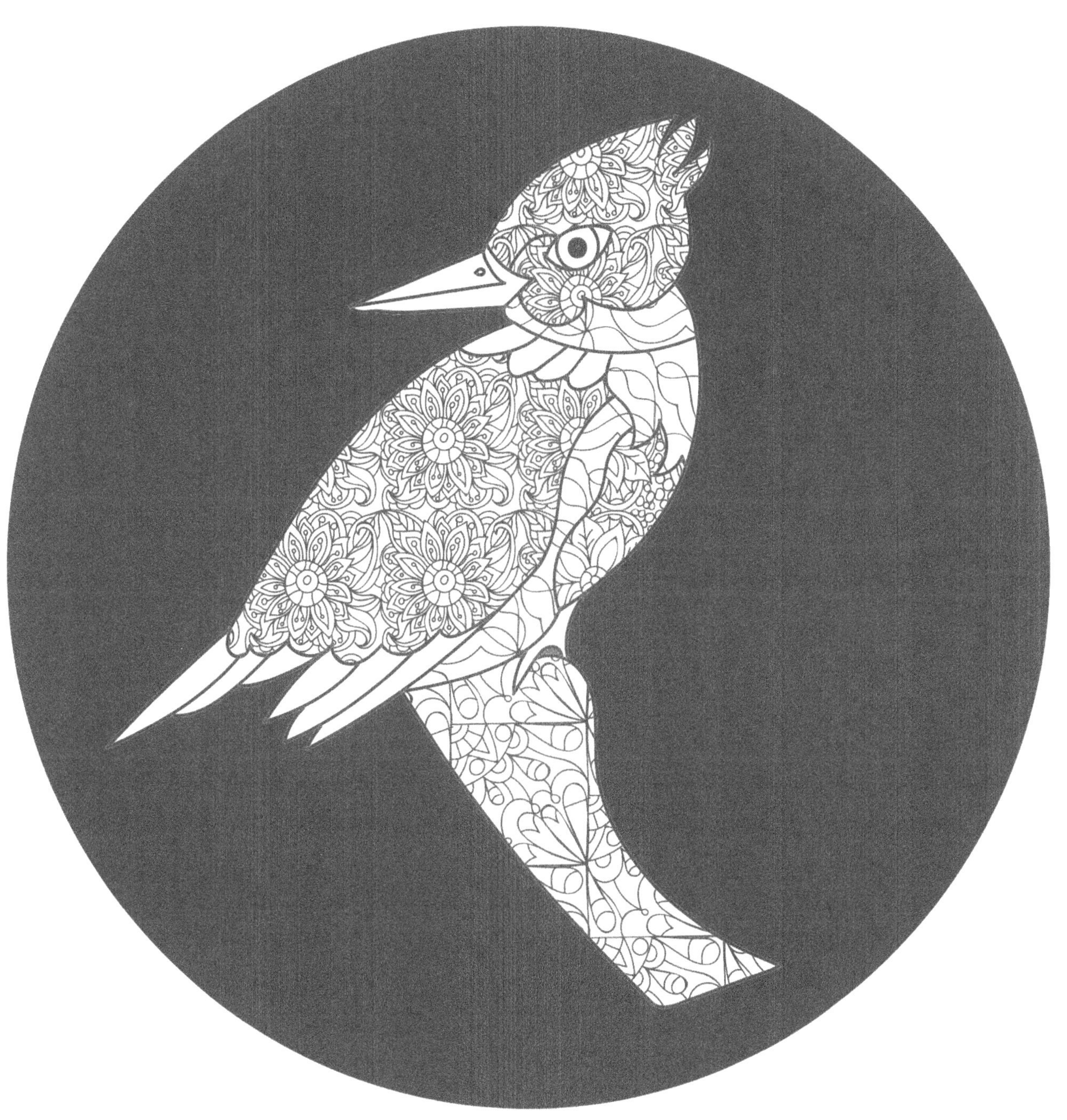

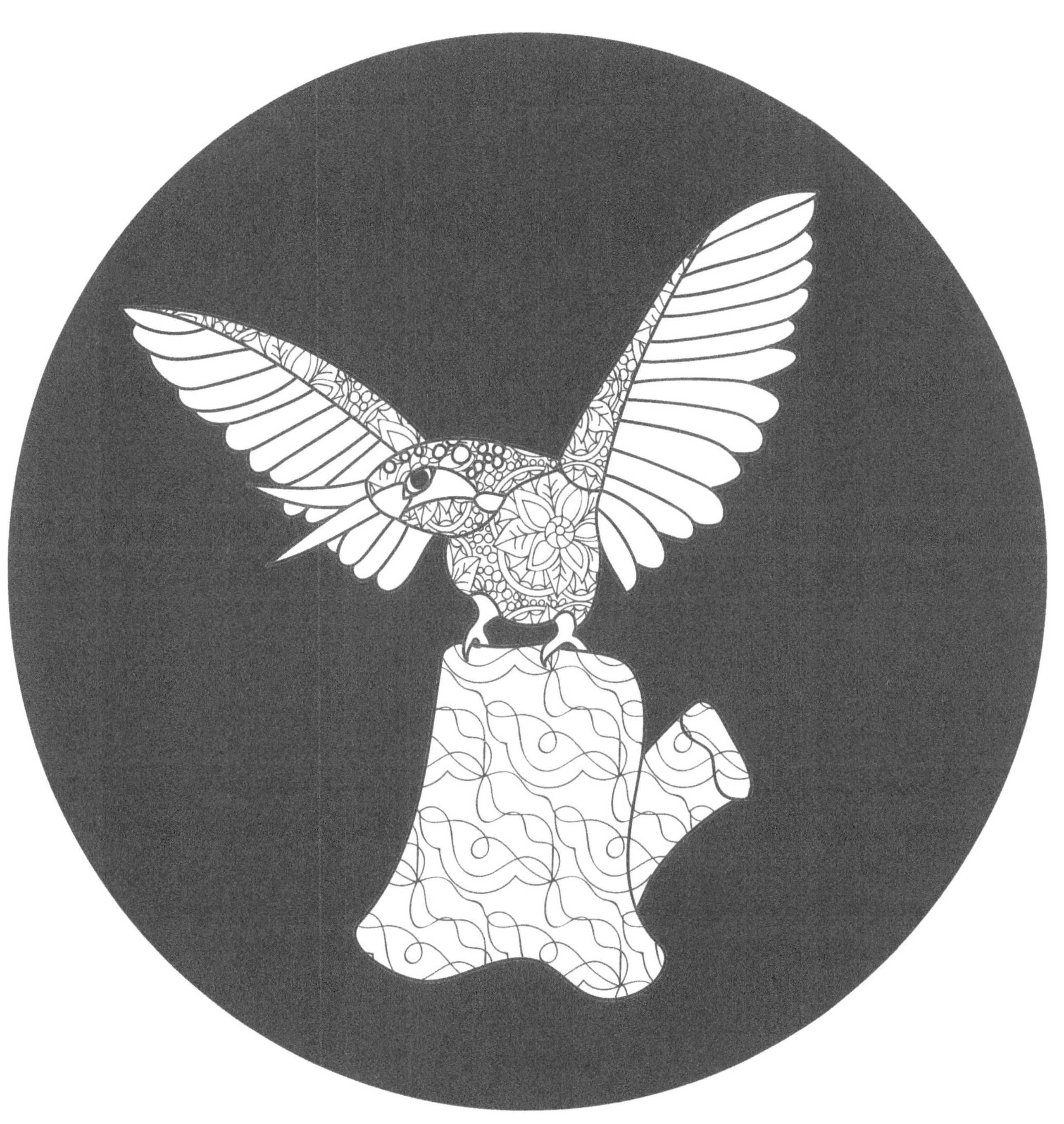

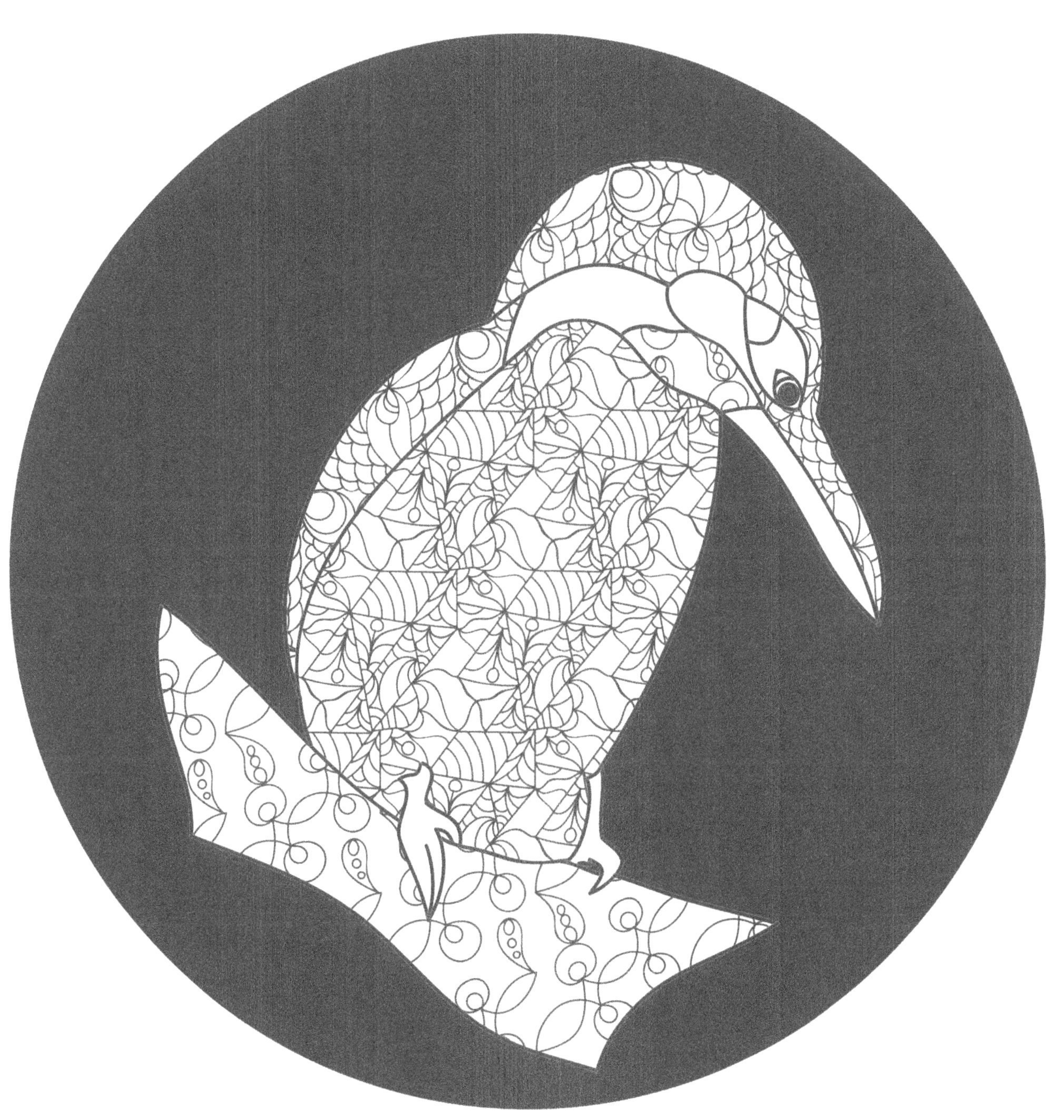

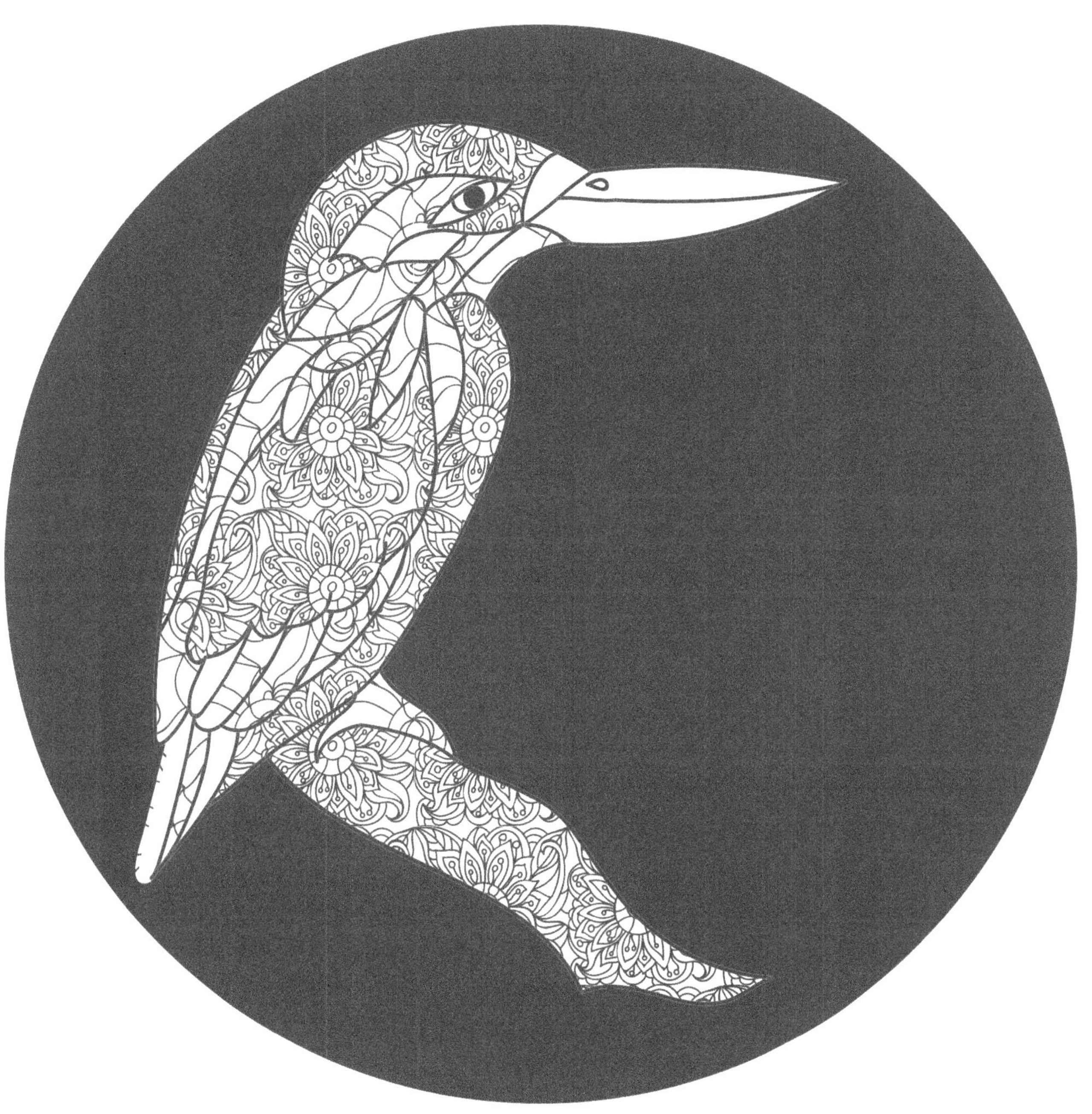

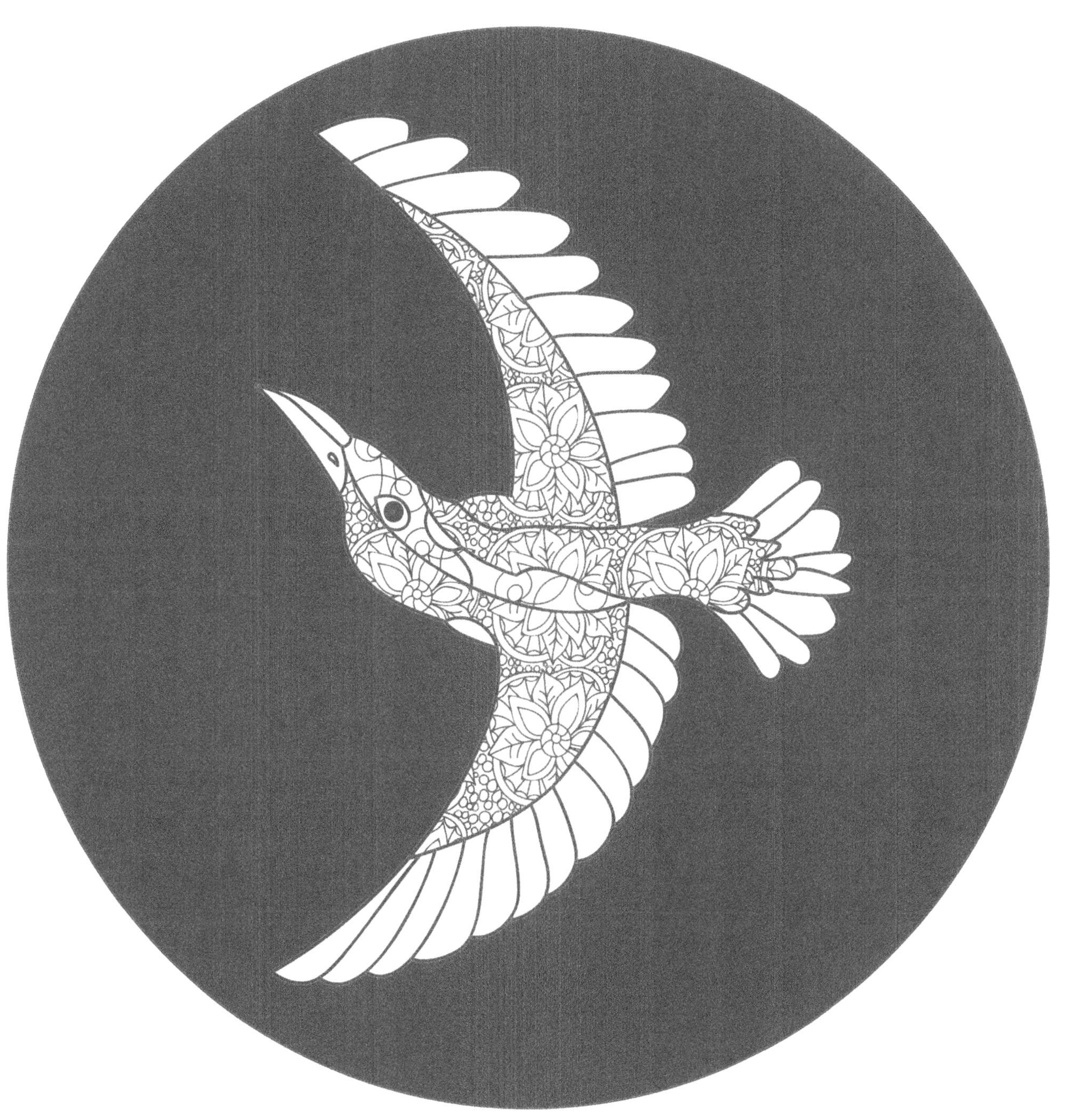

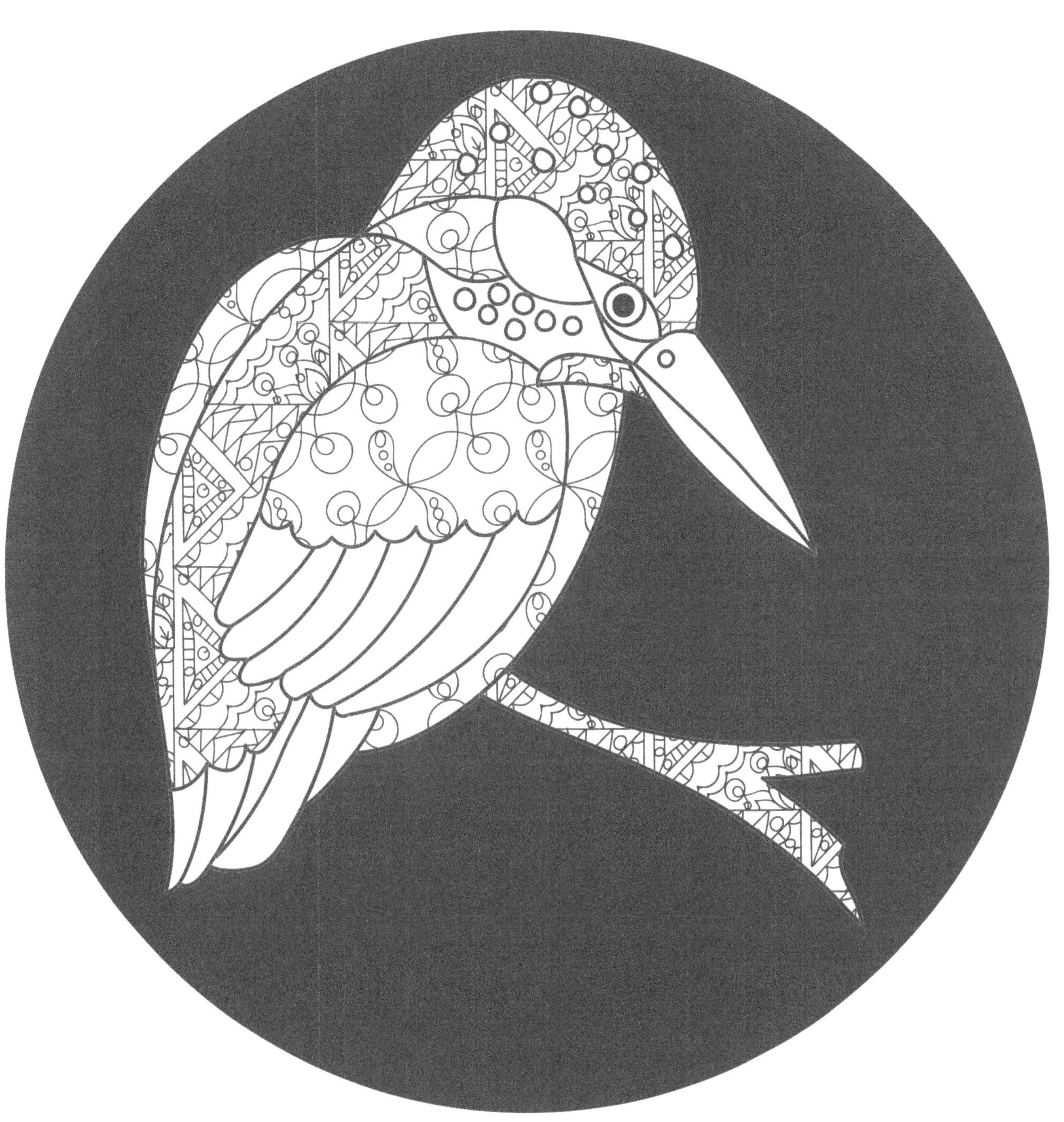

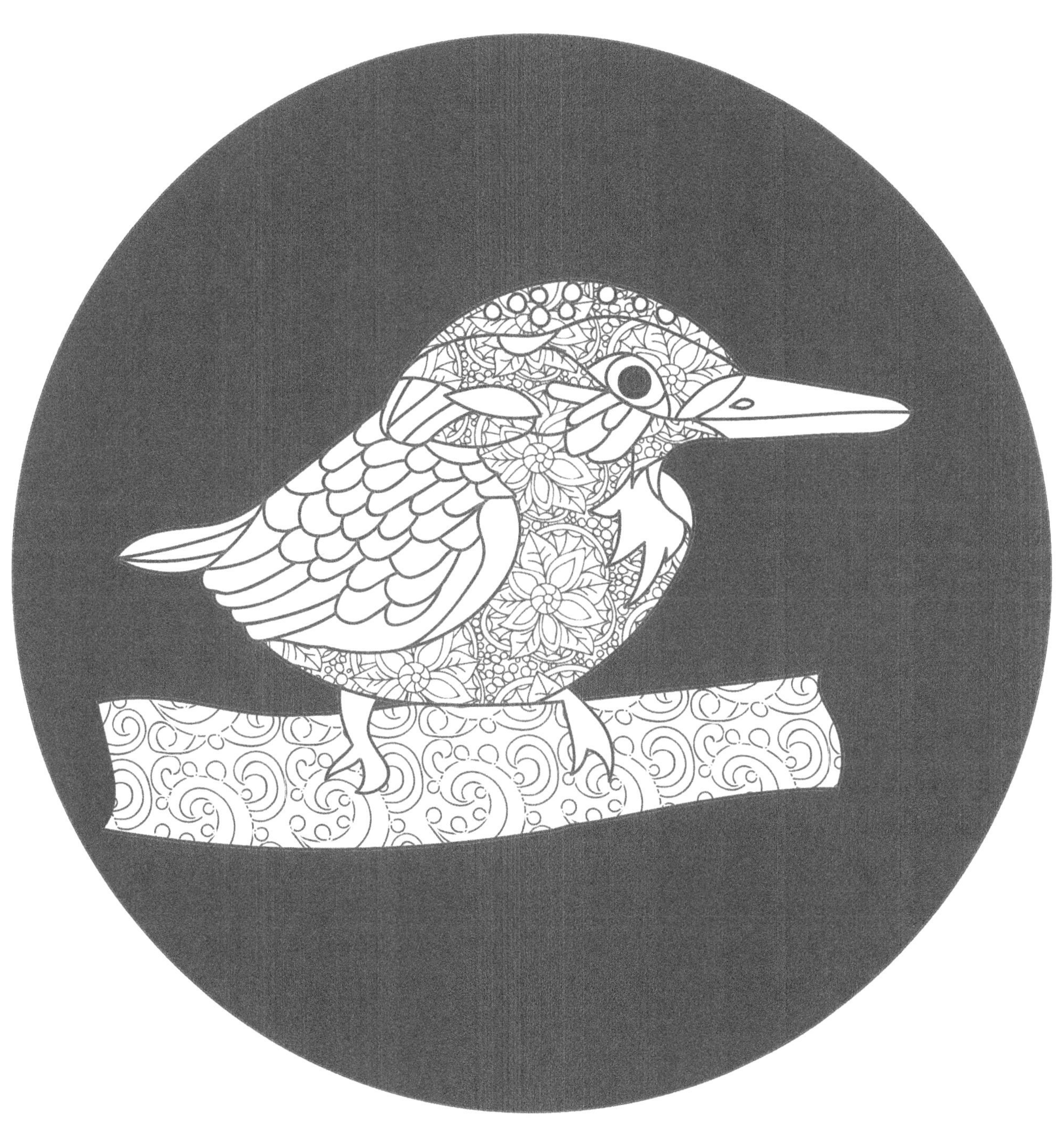

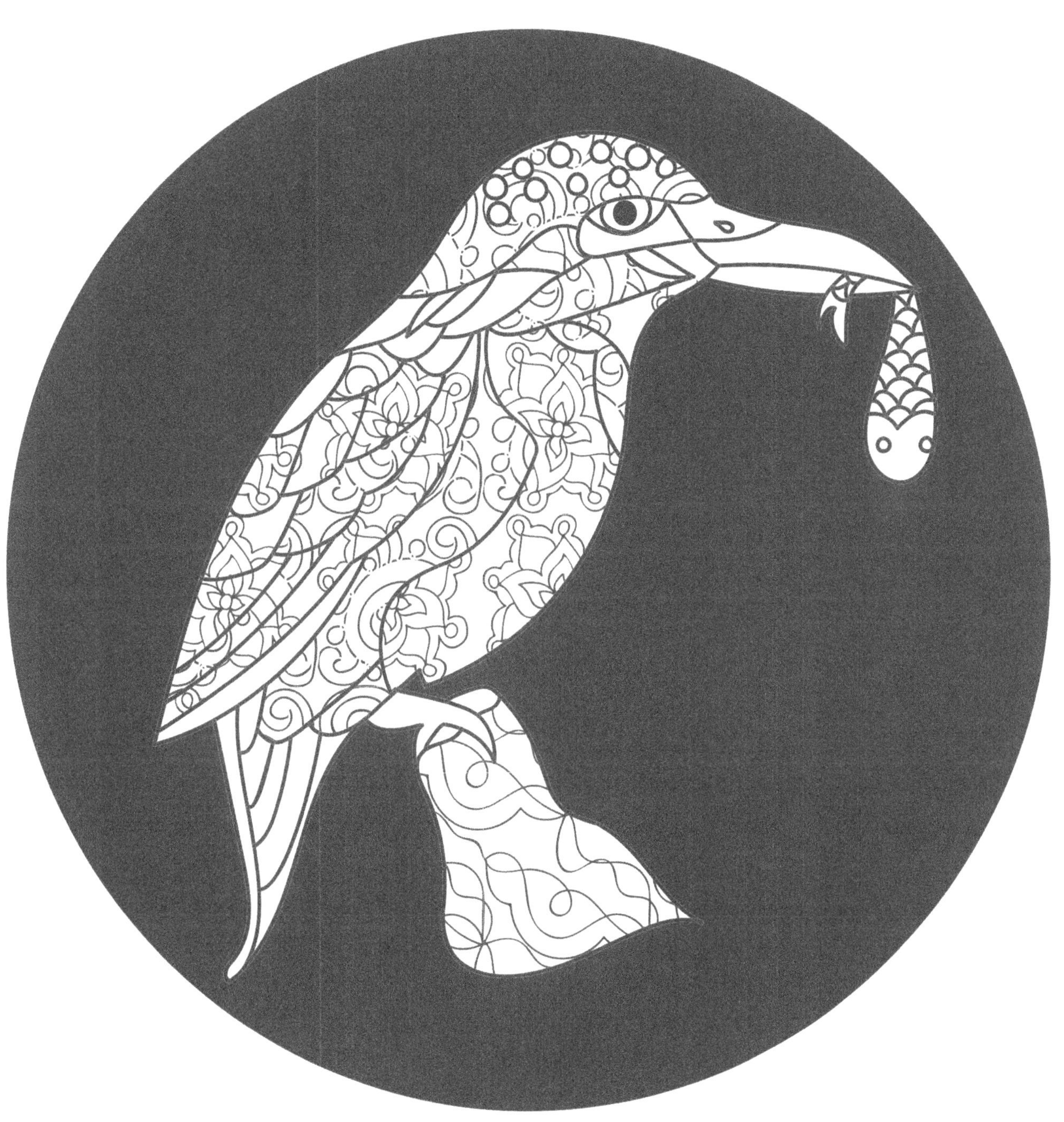

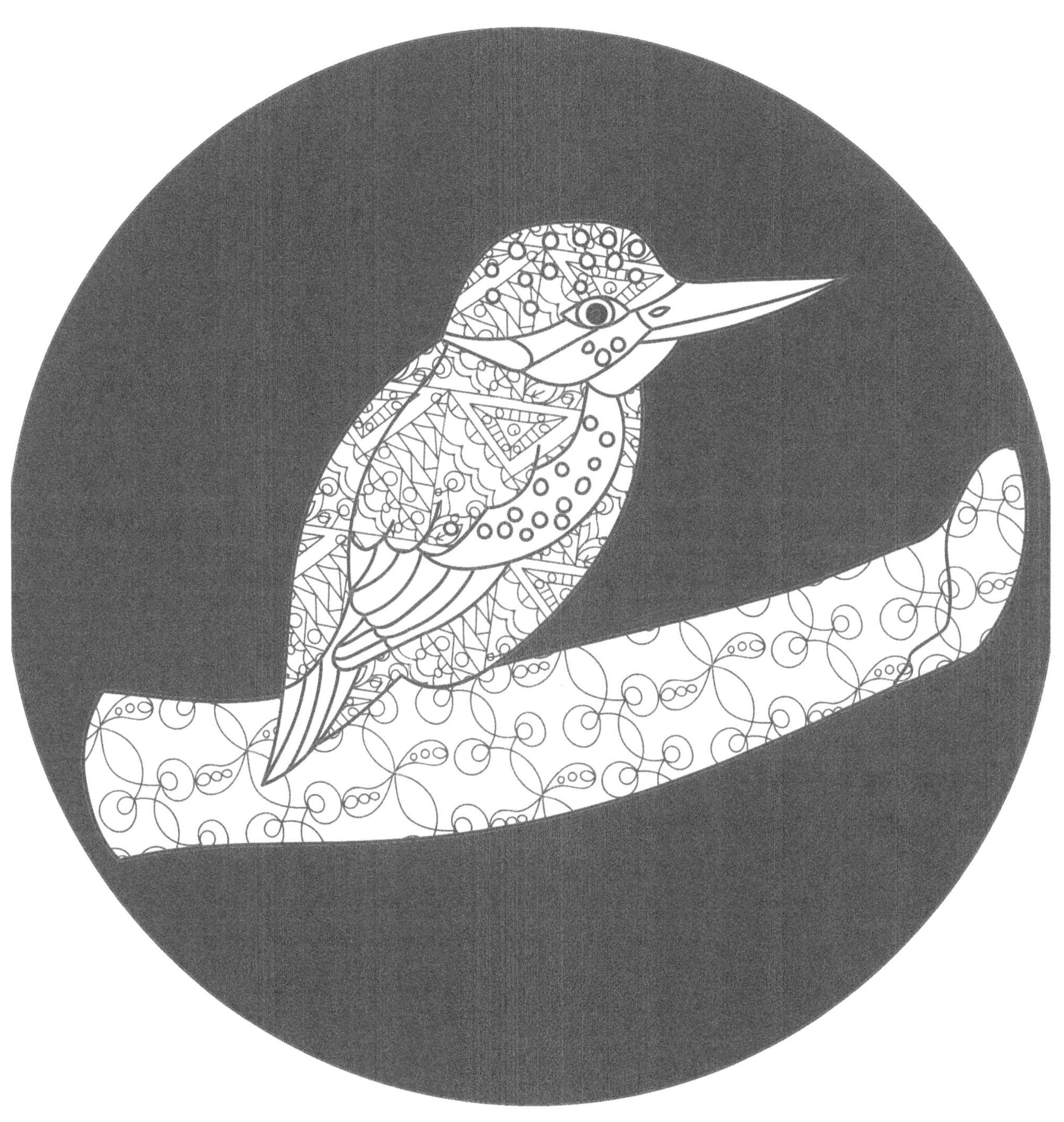

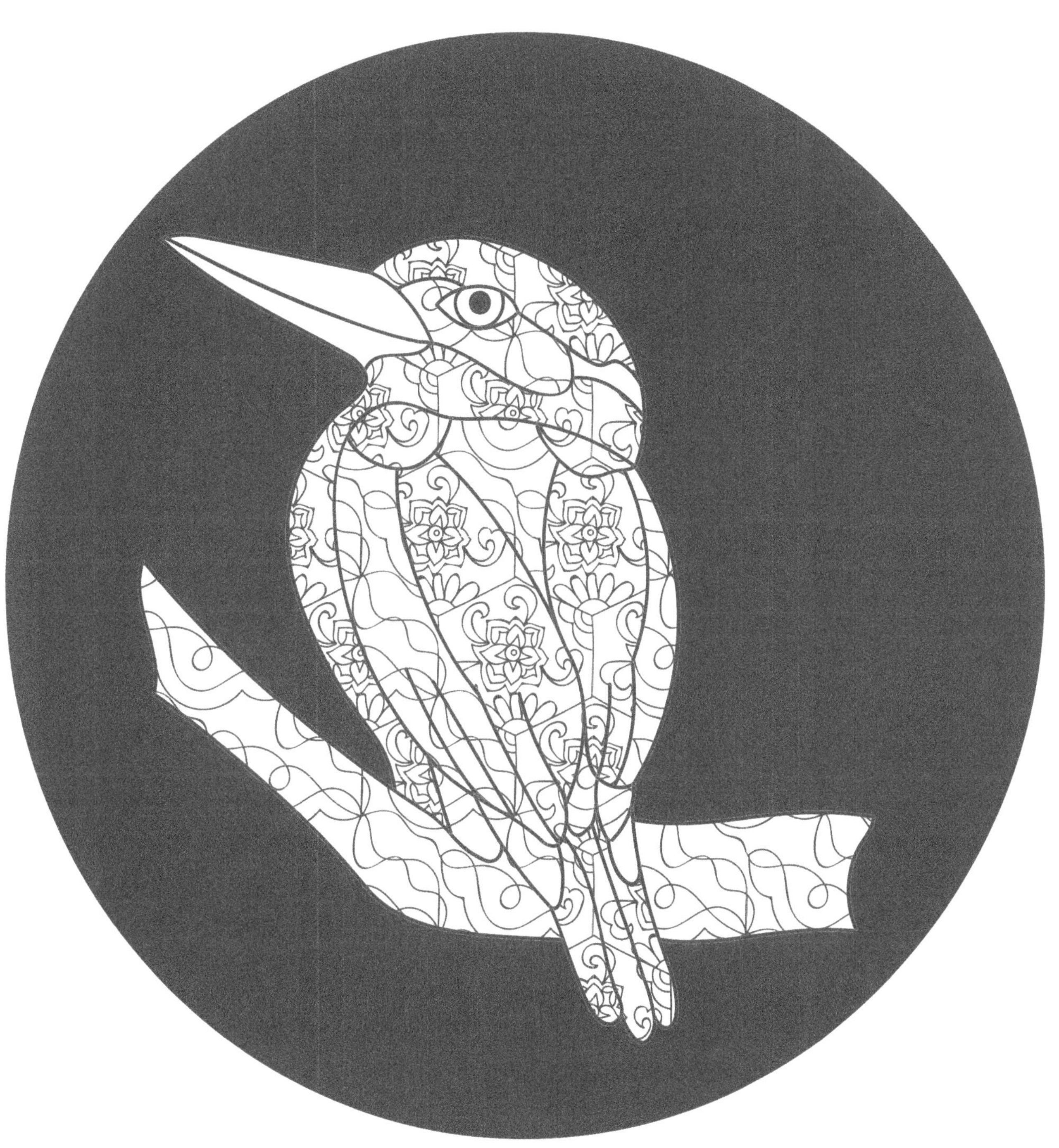

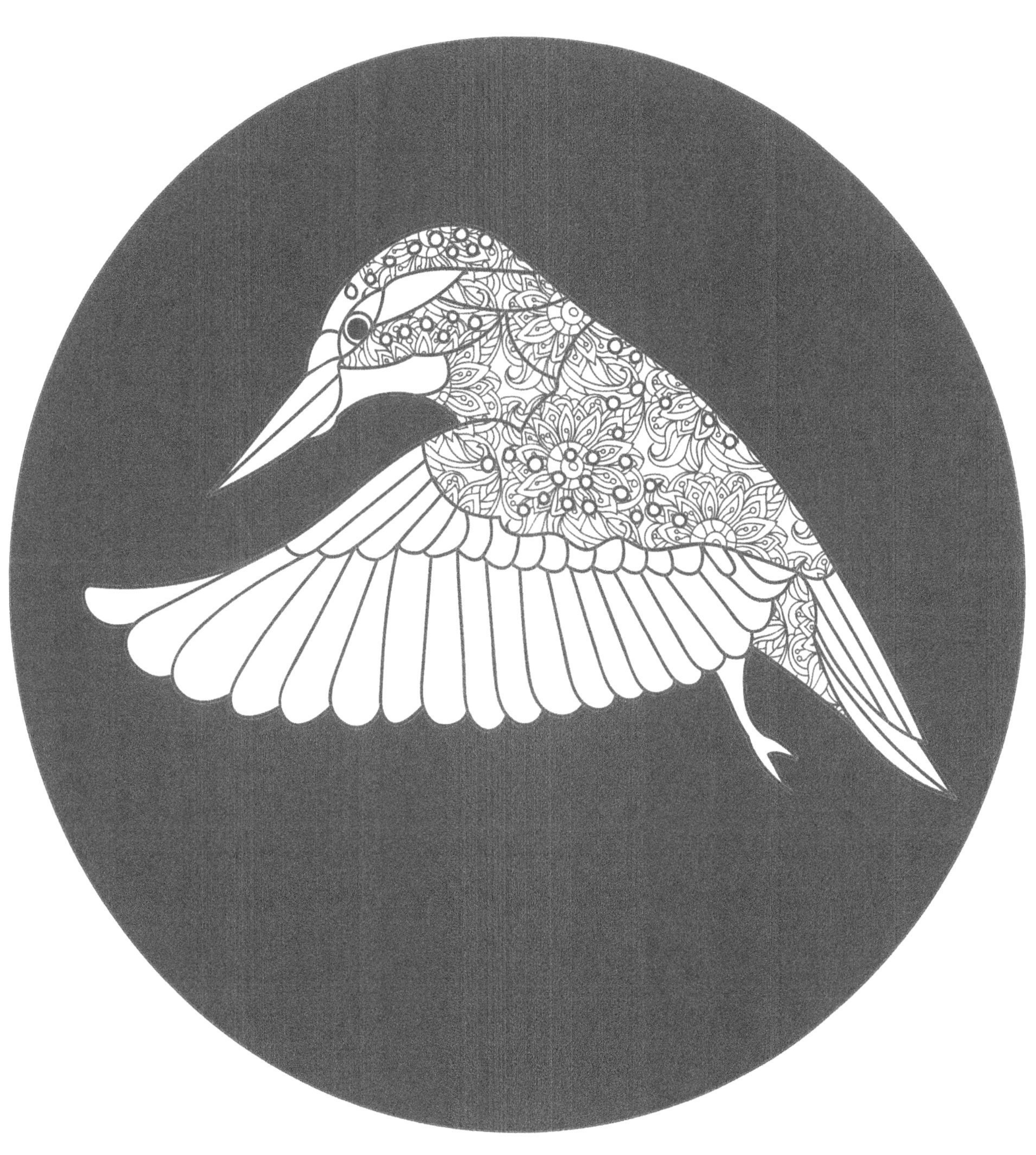

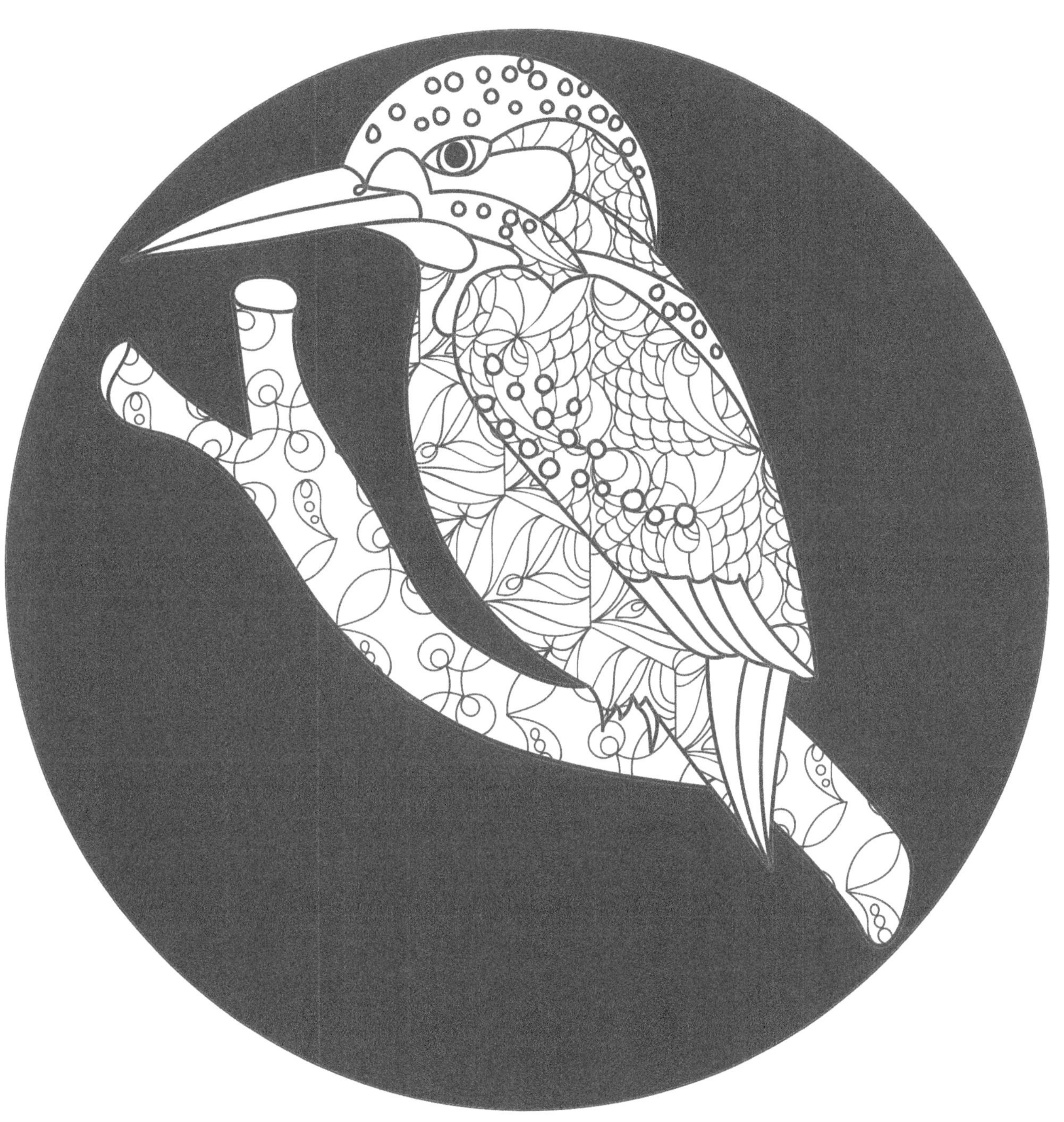

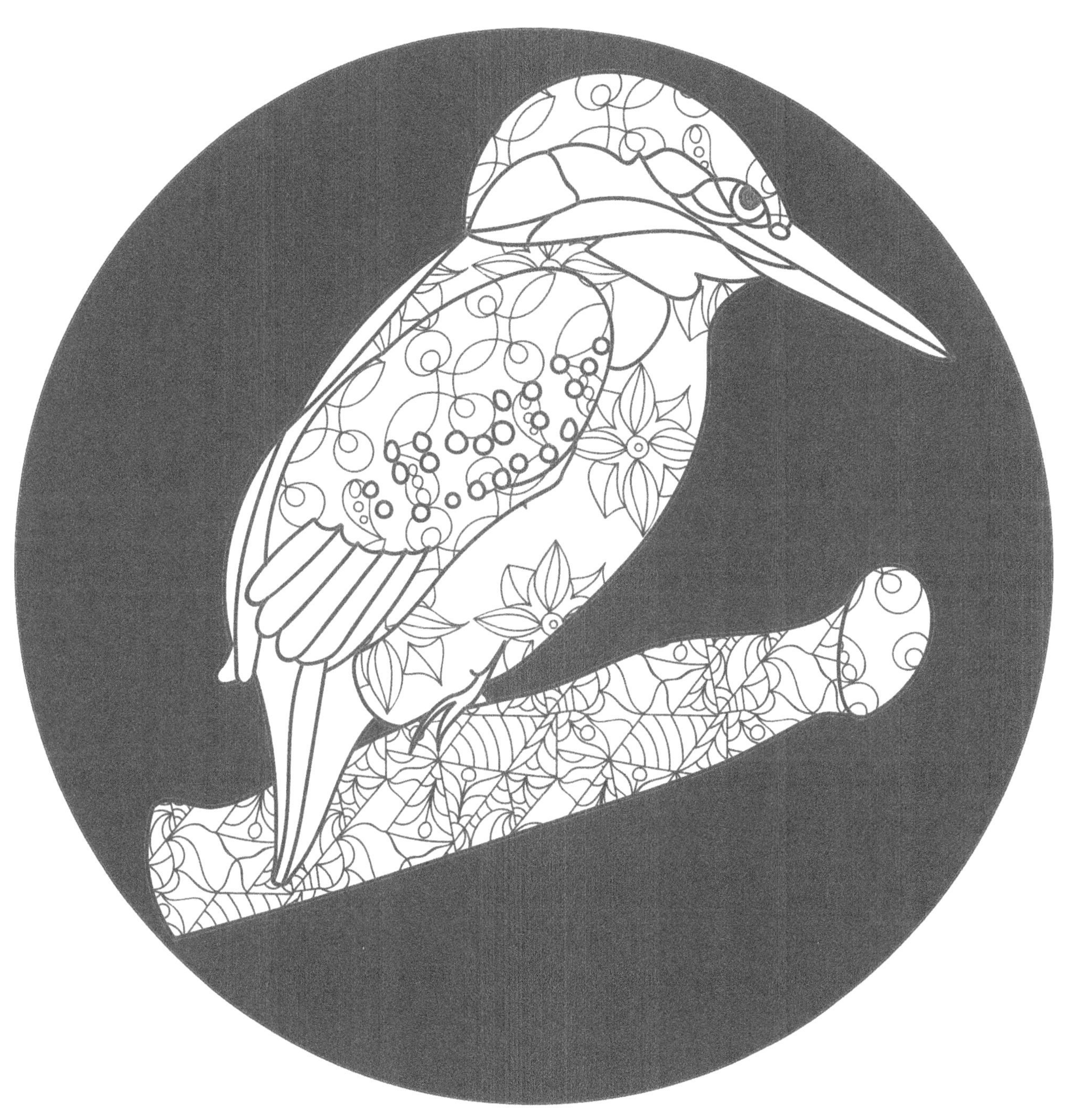

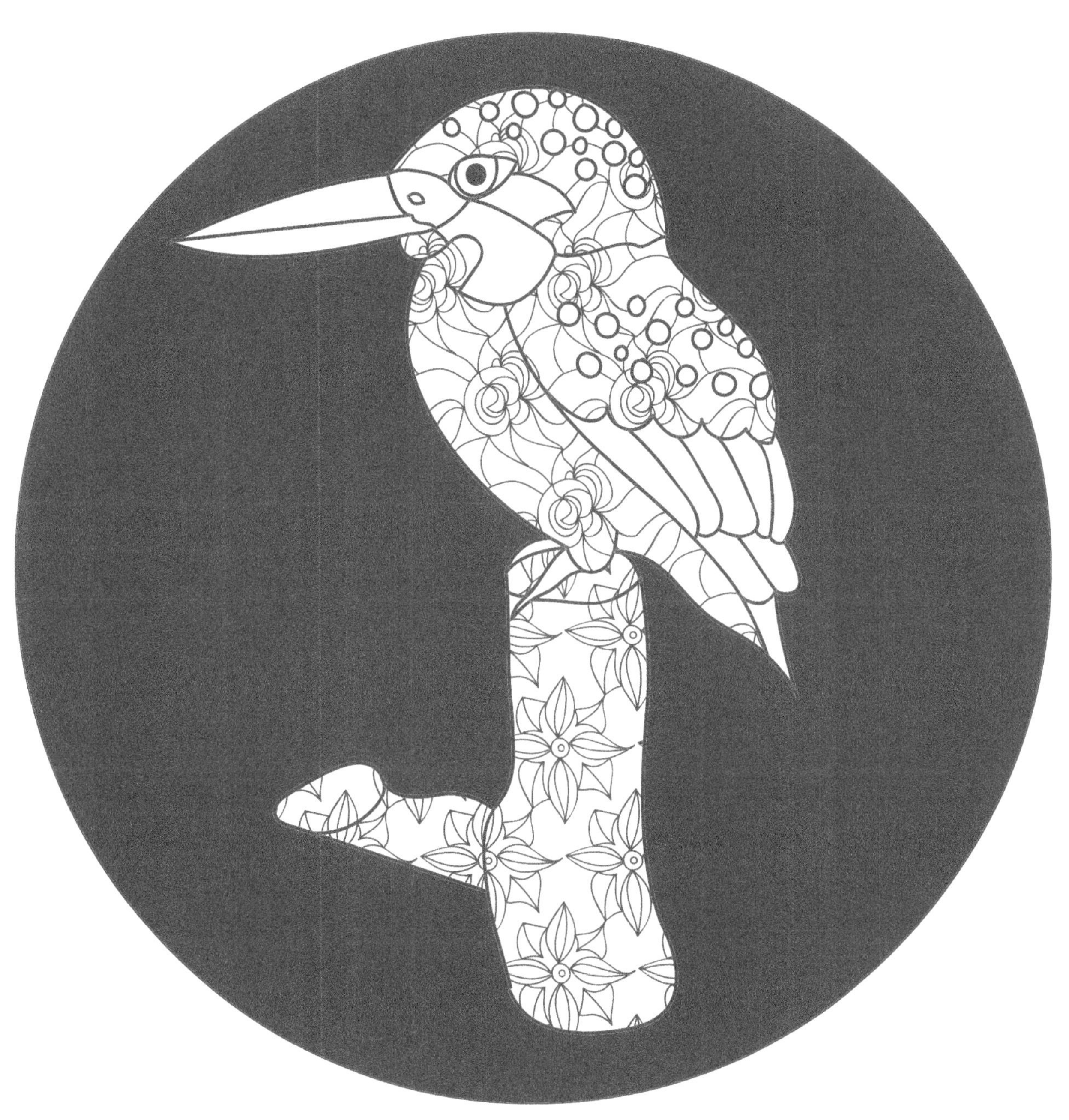

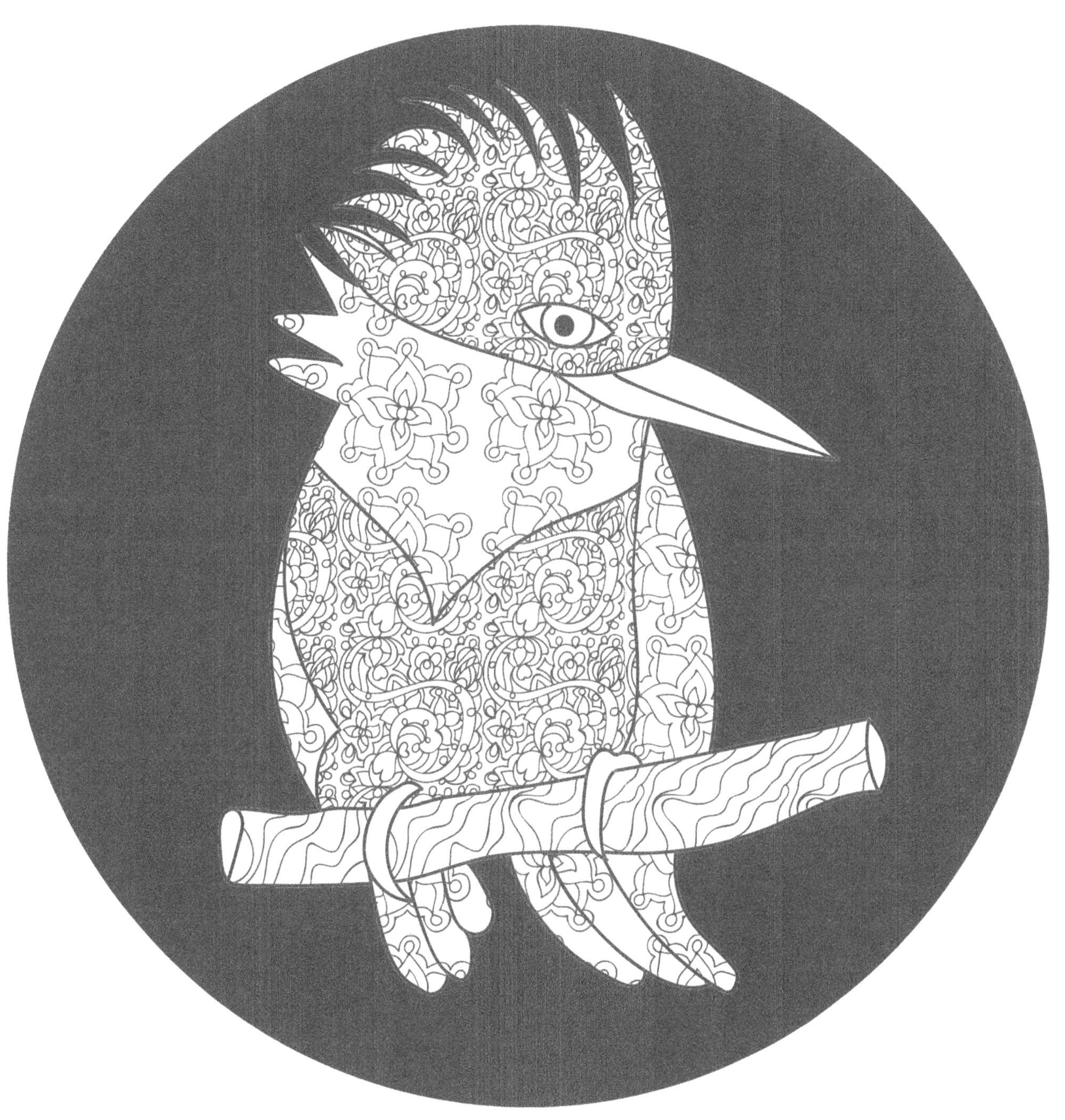

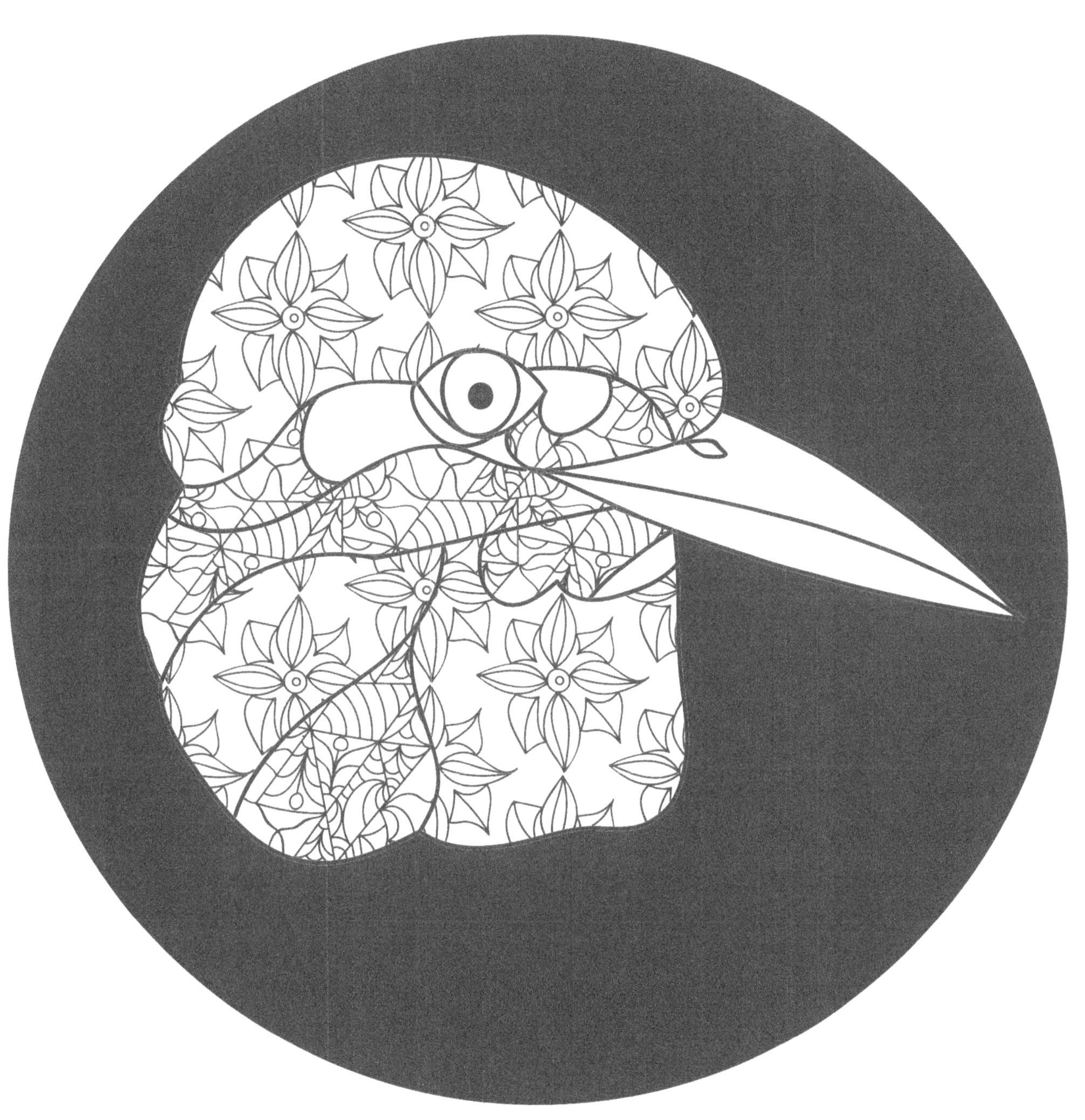

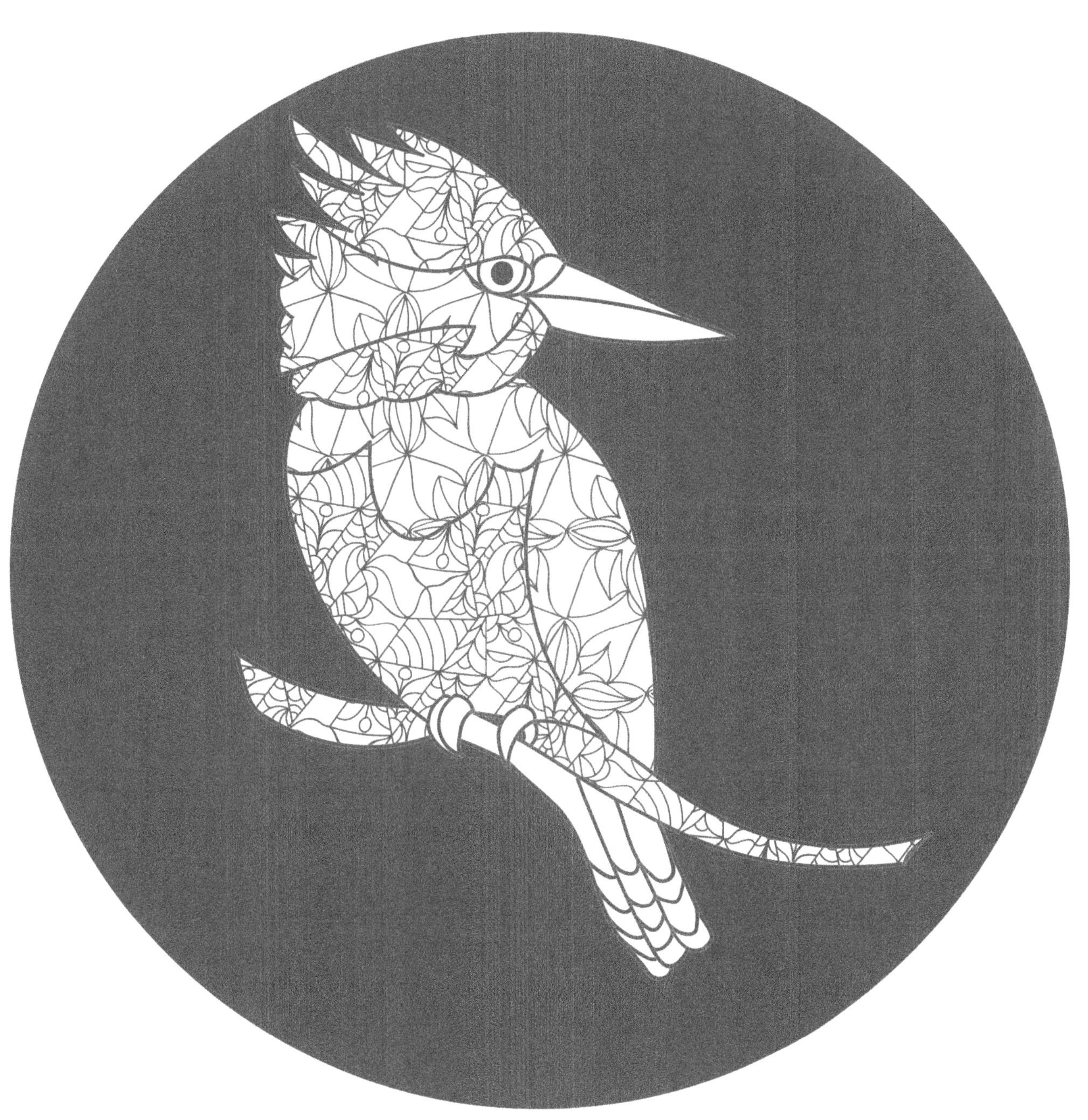

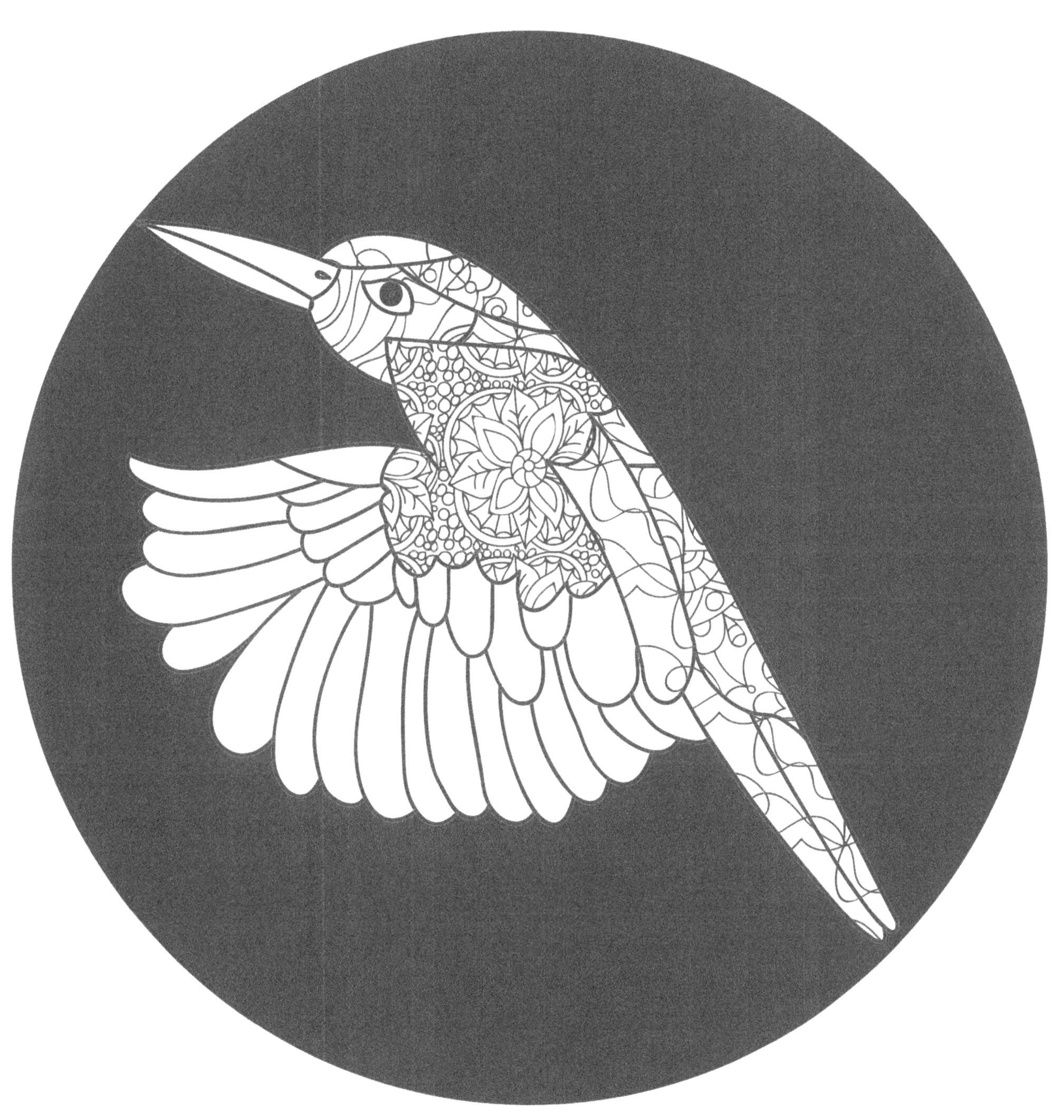

COLOR TEST PAGE

COLOR TEST PAGE

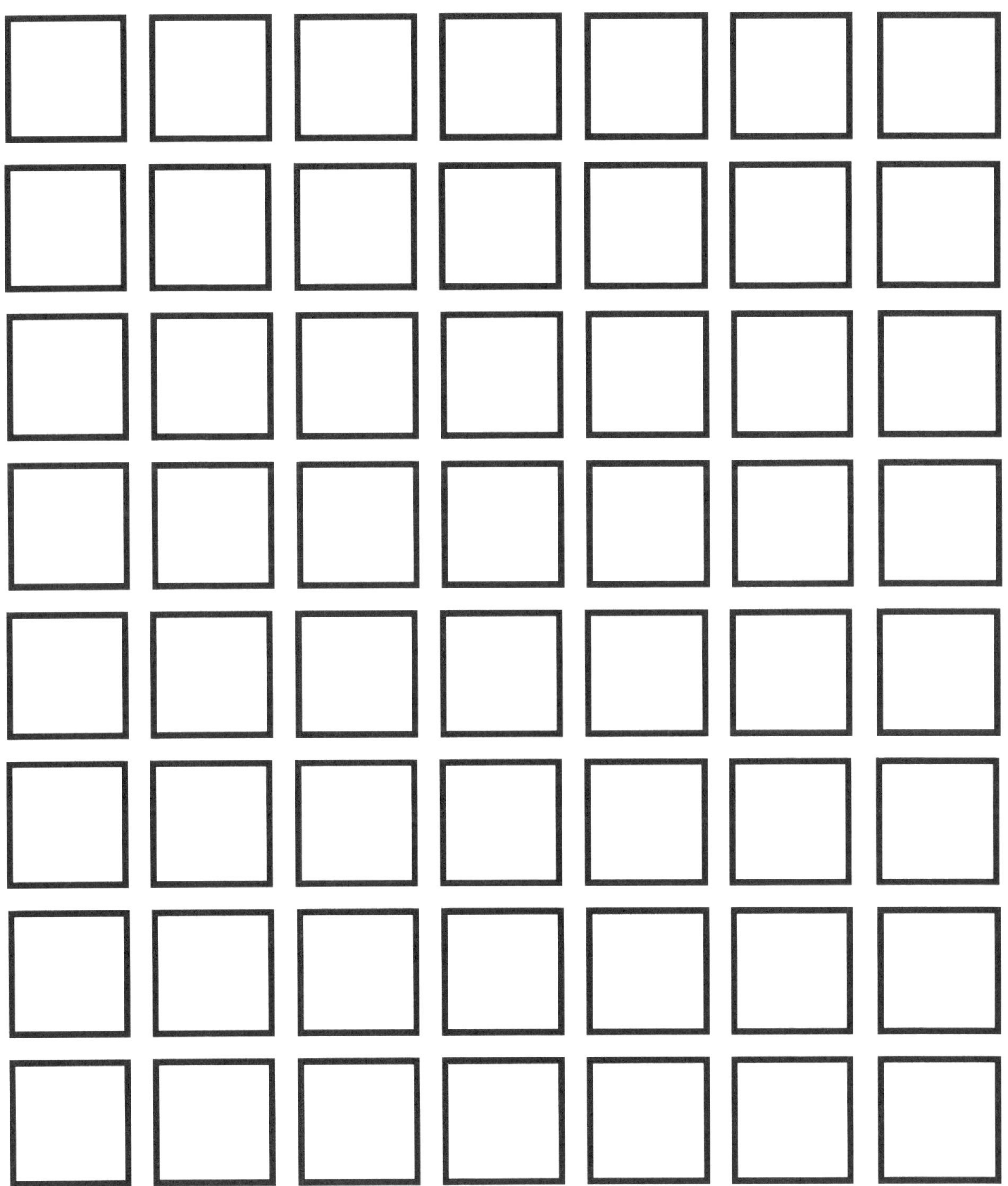